# THE UNFAIR ADVANTAGE

## DIGITAL MARKETING PRINCIPLES THAT WILL EXPLODE THE GROWTH OF AN AUTO DEALERSHIP

## CHRIS J. MARTINEZ

J. JOSEPH GROUP

# CONTENTS

J. Joseph Group, LLC

ISBN: 978-0-9979314-8-8 (eBook)

ISBN: 978-0-9979314-9-5 (pbk)

Printed in the United States of America

# CONSULTING AND TRAINING

## CHRIS MARTINEZ

Chris Martinez has recently joined the board of The Automotive Partners (www.TheAutomotivePartners.com) with the intent of globally disrupting the automotive space.

He selectively speaks, coaches, and consults with auto dealerships to help them strategize and hone an effective and scalable marketing plan. If you're interested in learning more, please reach out to him via either of his websites: www.chrisjosephmartinez.com or www.TheAutoMiner.com

# DISCLAIMER

While the author has taken utmost effort to ensure the accuracy of the written content, all readers are advised to follow the information mentioned herein at their own risk. The author cannot be held responsible for any personal or commercial damage caused by misinterpretation of information. All readers are encouraged to seek professional advice when needed.

This book has been written for informational purposes only. Every effort has been made to make this book as complete and accurate as possible. However, there may be mistakes in typography or content. Also, this book provides information believed to be accurate only up to the publishing date. Therefore, this book should be used as a guide, not as the ultimate source.

The purpose of this book is to educate. The author and the publisher do not warrant that the information contained in this book is fully complete and shall not be responsible for any errors or omissions. The author and publisher shall have neither liability nor responsibility to any person or entity with respect to any loss or damage caused or alleged to be caused directly or indirectly by this book.

*For my wife, Veronica, and my kids, Jazmin, Janelle, Julianna, and Christian. Thank you for continuing to encourage me each and every day.*

# INTRODUCTION

I helped grow the Charles Maund Toyota dealership in Austin, Texas by approximately 680% in seven years. And yet, auto dealership marketing is not a career in which I ever saw myself or expected to find myself so passionate. In fact, it was never my intention to get into car sales at all! Nevertheless, life took the turns that life takes, and I sold a lot of vehicles and honed the art and science of dealership marketing at Charles Maund Toyota from 2011 until 2018.

When I started at Charles Maund, we were selling an average of 1,800 vehicles per year, and by 2018 that number had increased to 10,800 using a combination of digital and traditional marketing strategies. I assure you, if I can figure out how to so successfully grow a dealership through effective marketing strategies, you can figure out how to do the same with yours—regardless of your professional background, innate marketing skill set, or role within the dealership.

Whenever a business launches a new product or service, it's essential to spread the word. An effective advertising campaign informs customers of the availability of new products and services as well as the many ways they can benefit from them.

Regardless of industry, a marketing strategy is critical to gaining and retaining a greater market share of customers.

**Regardless of industry, a marketing strategy is critical to gaining and retaining a greater market share of customers.**

THE UNFAIR ADVANTAGE
- PRINCIPLES -

Generally speaking, the owner or general manager of a dealership is in charge of the dealership's marketing (at least at the highest strategic level). In order for me to learn more about this critical component of dealership growth, I was asked in 2011 to be our dealership's Internet Marketing Director, acting as the liaison to the marketing agencies and companies we were partnered with. As I dove in and learned more and more, I recognized that my unique knowledge of and experience with car dealerships could be an integral asset to these outside agencies when it came to generating successful dealership campaigns.

Dealerships rely on a variety of advertising and marketing tactics to find customers, retain those customers, and consistently increase overall sales. Print media used to be the most powerful medium used to reach customers. People would spend their Sunday morning with a cup of coffee and the Classified Ads section of newspapers or rely on word-of-mouth in order to purchase their next vehicle. Later, they turned to radio, television, and cable TV advertising.

Times have again changed. From bookstores to grocery

stores to car dealerships, every industry now has an online presence and does a majority of their advertising online because that's where the customers are. Technology has introduced (and continues to introduce) a huge variety of options which, when employed correctly, allow dealerships to expand and retain their customer base more quickly, efficiently, and cost effectively than ever before.

General marketing principles haven't changed in decades because human psychology hasn't changed. Marketing platforms have changed, however, and continue to do so. Therefore, dealerships (as well as every other type of business) must take the same marketing concepts that have worked for decades and figure out how to best apply them to the newest platforms. So many dealerships I speak with are doing next to nothing in the area of digital marketing. Or, they're doing a lot of stuff but it's haphazard and, therefore, ineffective.

The reason most dealerships' marketing efforts fall short is that their overall foundation is shaky. Because the majority don't set an effective strategy in place to make the most of their marketing campaigns, businesses tend to invest an unnecessarily large portion of their revenue into advertising, which eventually reduces their profit. It's entirely possible to make marketing and advertising campaigns even more lucrative (and fun) by establishing a proper strategy that's tied to a set of proven principles and then committing to carrying out all promotional campaigns accordingly.

Developing an effective marketing strategy is a dealership's most pressing challenge. The purpose of this book is to assist with that. Marketing campaigns are essential for any business, and with the help of a practical marketing strategy, your dealership will be able to make the most of your financial resources (and avoid overspending, which happens far more frequently than necessary).

Over the course of my seven years at Charles Maund Toyota, we developed a solid marketing strategy that allowed us to promote our business and achieve our goals with ease, year after year. I'm excited to share the principles underlying that strategy with you so that you, too, can propel your dealership to stand out from the competition and thrive. I've acquired a vast amount of knowledge when it comes to what to focus on, what *not* to focus on, how to maximize a limited budget and personnel resources, and how to scale effective campaigns.

While I'll cover some of the specific advertising and marketing strategies that have worked best for us and for other dealerships I've worked with (regardless of brand), the detailed tactics themselves aren't the cornerstone of success. The principles are. If all of social media, voice mail, direct mail, and banner ads disappear tomorrow, the principles are what will help you pivot and successfully apply them to whatever new platform has popped up in their place. Those principles are:

- Branding is the new selling
- Humanize the Dealership
- Provide Value to Customers and Community
- Know Who's In Charge
- Strategy Wins (Even When It Loses)
- Measure the Data

I believe Bill Gates was the first to say, "I choose a lazy person to do a hard job. Because a lazy person will find an easy way to do it." I think that, perhaps, I'm the kind of "lazy person" to whom he was referring. I put in a lot of work; I'm not afraid to work. So I'm not lazy in that sense, but I definitely want to find the easiest way to do something and then see how fast I can multiply and scale that effort. Everything in my life has always seemed far less complicated when I'm focused. I find that most people overthink things. In grade school, I was always the first one to finish my work. I'd get a 98% on a test, and it would be a stupid mistake that kept me from a perfect score. I knew that if I just slowed down I'd get 100%, but thought, "Well, 98% is pretty good."

I hung around with the wrong crowd from ages 13 until 18. They were good people, but they made bad choices. Thinking back, I put myself in some pretty bad situations—the kind that could have landed me in jail for a long time. It's still scary to think about. I didn't even show up at school much in high school. My senior year, I only showed up for the first two months, at which point the court ordered my mom to be at the school *with* me to ensure that I went and stayed until end of day. She literally had to sit outside my class to make sure I didn't leave. Even when I turned 18 and tried to drop out, the judge said, "No, you're going to stay."

Toward the end of that year, I went to Mexico and got into a horrible fight. I was in the hospital for about a week, and my aunt called and asked if I wanted to stay with her in Las Vegas and finish school. I figured it was time to get my life together, so I did. I focused intently from 6:30am to 7:00pm every single day finishing out high school. I got straight A's and finally graduated after a grand total of five years. After graduation, I returned to El Paso to attend college. I was somehow passing my classes, and people couldn't understand how because they were actually listening yet were still completely confused. One day, one of my buddies from high school showed up and convinced me to go out instead of attending class. That was my last day of college. It wasn't the wisest choice, but I met my wife shortly thereafter and she helped me become a better person. When she asked me about my goals, a light bulb turned on. I wondered, *What am I doing?* No one had ever asked me those kinds of questions before, and they challenged me to take control of my future.

Those first few years were tough. No one had taught me how to make money. I knew that in order to get a good job I had to go back to school. Another option was to work construction with my uncle. I knew I could make money in construction because I knew the craft. I flew to Las Vegas with my brother after he told me about a car dealership that was trying to recruit him. I went to the interview instead of my brother and got the job. That's where it all started. I couldn't believe how much money you could make selling cars. I learned so much at my first dealership about what was actually possible in the industry.

As much as I sometimes wish I could erase the early years of my life, they helped me understand that there's no reason to do things the wrong way. You can do them the right way and win without cheating. At the time, there was no real way for me to get around my situation. It's a different way of life when you know you're getting evicted every two months, or you're coming home and there's no electricity or running water, or you have to go to church and wait in line to get expired food, or you don't have a jacket because you outgrew yours and your mom can't afford to buy a new one so you just wear multiple shirts layered over one another. That was the environment I grew up in, and I always thought, "There's got to be a better way." I'd cut my neighbors' yards to make a bit of money to get what we needed. It was simple survival. Being a dad now, I want to be a positive role model for my kids, to teach them how to do things the right way and know that there are higher standards to aspire to. That's what gets me going everyday: being a better role model for the next generation. I'm trying to do things the right way; no shortcuts. My goal is to win, without cheating.

Just recently there was the whole Volkswagon scandal about trying to cheat on emissions. There are simply a lot of people who take the easy way, but that doesn't make it right. That was my main message to my team at Charles Maund—and believe me, I had to let go of a lot of people on my team because they insisted on taking shortcuts. Why take a shortcut when it's the wrong thing to do? No car deal is worth your reputation or your career. You have to live with yourself and be able to sleep at night. Too many people are trying to cut a fast path to success by doing things the wrong way.

For example, salespeople simply have to do a better job of

closing the customer more quickly. Yes, better technology will help facilitate the basics and help salespeople convert prospects into buyers, but even if I generate a lead through Facebook, if I have a purely SMS-based conversation with a customer, I'll likely lose him or her. I'll be primarily talking to myself. Lead nurturing is a real thing! Lots of times, when salespeople get a lead, they'll just send a brief text or email instead of sending a message that compels the customer to pick up the phone and call.

Nurturing the lead requires more personality when communicating with the customer to the extent that he or she gets excited about the possibility of purchasing a car from you. The first dealership that gets in contact with the customer wins. What happens with leads is, for example, if True Car sends a customer's information to three dealerships, you end up with three dealerships essentially fighting for that customer. Some dealers take 10 or 20 minutes to reach out to that customer. Generally, the first dealership to reach out wins. What we've built and continue to build with our application, The AutoMiner (which I'll discuss in more detail in a bit), is essentially going to facilitate the conversions increase that dealerships are looking for.

On average, a dealership closes between 10 and 12 percent of their leads. With the help of technology we've been able to stay at 18-20%. The minute that we capture a lead, we can initiate a text message automatically, letting the customer know that we have what he's looking for and to give us a call. The customer is initiating the contact by giving their contact information through Facebook, and we have a disclaimer letting them know that they are going to receive a text message. As long as they opt-in for that, they'll get a text that also gives them the option to unsubscribe. Compliance is key and every state may be different so do your homework.

In addition to proven marketing strategies for auto dealerships, I've spent the last three years developing and refining The AutoMiner to help dealerships specifically more efficiently and effectively retain their sales and service customers. Important to note up front is that Charles Maund Toyota was able to generate over $168,000 in sales and service revenue simply by increasing our efficiency and reducing our costs through use of The AutoMiner combined with our unique understanding of effective dealership marketing.

Slow and steady wins the race. Tony Robbins has what is arguably the best quote on time management and expectations: "Most people overestimate what they can do in a year, and they underestimate what they can do in two or three decades."

So buckle your seatbelt (pun intended), and let's get you on your way to an effective, principle-based, scalable, and profitable marketing strategy.

# BRANDING IS THE NEW SELLING

Toyota as a whole does a great job of branding its product as reliable and dependable, but as an individual dealership, it's critical to assess how well you are marketing yourself, separate from the global brand. At Charles Maund, we had to constantly ask ourselves, "Are we, as a dealership, effectively branding what makes us different from any other Toyota dealership?"

DEALERSHIP BRANDING TIP

**Who are you, what do you do, and how are you different?**

THE UNFAIR ADVANTAGE

Who are you, what do you do, and how are you different? As simple as they sound, these three questions represent the core of branding and being able to answer them in detail provides the foundation for a successful marketing strategy. Your long-term growth—financial and otherwise—largely depends on the overall reputation of your brand. The focus must be not only on the vehicle brand (Toyota, Audi, Mercedes, etc,) but your specific *dealership's* brand. If customers trust your brand, you'll have an edge in a highly competitive market. A key focus of your marketing strategy, therefore, should be building awareness of and trust in your brand.

## BECOME A HOUSEHOLD NAME

Every dealership wishes to become a household name, especially in their general geographic region. In our case, we wanted to see and hear the words "Charles Maund Toyota" as often as possible. That way, anytime a local consumer was considering a Toyota vehicle, they immediately thought of Charles Maund Toyota. Think about your local accident attorneys. A catchy jingle (often including their phone number) likely comes to mind. When you need new workout apparel, fishing or other outdoor equipment, you almost immediately think of a specific store to go to to satisfy each need. This is because you've learned to associate fishing gear with Bass Pro Shop, for example, or workout shorts with Sports Authority. When I need new suits, I go to Brooks Brothers. When I need almost anything else, I go to Nordstrom. When you automatically think of a specific brand the minute you realize you're in need of something, it's because that brand has cemented itself in your mind as the obvious solution in that area. They continue to meet or exceed your expectations, and until they no longer do, they likely won't be replaced.

The task of becoming this ingrained in a consumer's mind, however, isn't as easy as it may initially sound. For starters, you'll need to create ad campaigns capable of catching the attention of your target audience. This is where the process begins, and beginning properly is critical. If you start throwing darts against a wall that doesn't even have a dart board hanging on it, you're unnecessarily wasting time and money (and darts). If you create a great campaign that catches the attention of people who have no interest in purchasing a new car, or who are unable to afford any of the vehicles on your lot, you've wasted precious time and money. In order to ensure that this doesn't happen, you need to be extremely clear on who your target audience is. It's also important to note that you'll have different target audiences for different ad campaigns.

Many businesses spend time promoting their products and services before they promote their brand as a whole. I know brands and businesses are eager to start seeing results in the form of increased sales, but trust me, setting a strong foundation by marketing your brand first is the key to selling far more products and services with far greater ease down the line. I always recommend that dealerships build and market their brand first *and then* attract customers to try out their vehicles as well as other products and services.

Given the availability of social media, which has produced some of the most cost-effective platforms yet when it comes to marketing, it's easier than ever for businesses to carry out effective marketing campaigns intended to build trust and rapport with consumers. This less-expensive barrier to entry also greatly increases the competition, so it's important to take every precaution to ensure that you stand out in a sea of marketing campaigns that are all fighting for consumers' attention.

If a customer searches online for a Toyota dealership, for example, he may discover that there are several of them within a 30-mile radius. You need to quickly determine how your dealership can stand out from that competition. One way to do that is to focus on customer support and ensure that the support you offer is far better than that of nearby dealerships. This will not only efficiently attract customers, it will assist you in retaining them. Be proactive in answering customers' questions and solving their problems, especially in public forums.

## BRAND AMBASSADORS

One of the approaches we successfully used to brand Charles Maund Toyota was partnering with Brand Ambassadors. Brand Ambassadors are social media influencers who the dealership allowed to borrow a car for a period of time. Those influencers then post regularly on their favorite social media platforms and tie in a current activity to the vehicle they're driving as well as to our dealership. (For example, "Hanging out in the Charles Maund Toyota lobby while I get my oil changed! Great service, plus free donuts!")

Our approach was to identify local influencers with 50k-100k authentic followers who are also predominantly local. After all, if an influencer resides in Austin but the majority if his or her followers live in the Northeast, we aren't likely to be a convenient choice for them when it comes time to purchase a vehicle. Admittedly, it's challenging to identify hard data that indicate how well this approach works, but in our experience, the overall goal is to increase the frequency with which our dealership gets out in front of people.

It's also critical to look for Brand Ambassadors who have authentic engagement with real fans (not robots). These days, it's easier than ever to buy fans. Many of the companies that provide this service are filling follower counts with fake users. Those users aren't interacting with an influencer, and if they are, they aren't *genuinely* interacting. They're perhaps programmed to "like" every fifth post, but they aren't paying attention, and no one is paying attention to them. It's no different from shouting your message into a deep (and empty) canyon.

Part of our agreement with Brand Ambassadors was that

they had to tag both myself and the dealership in every post. This allowed me to monitor who was posting what, and it also gave prospective customers an obvious way to reach out to someone at the dealership. I'd receive random texts from time to time asking if I could find someone a certain car. I didn't even know how I knew the person texting me. He wasn't a previous customer, so it was certainly possible that he or she was interested in a Toyota, saw one of our Brand Ambassadors posts on social media, and in that moment thought, "I wonder if they have a new RAV4?" Within five minutes, I could let them know that we had it, and they'd be on their way to the dealership to see it. Sometimes, a Brand Ambassador's follower would see the BA's car in a post and reach out to the influencer directly to ask where they got it.

It's important not to have your Brand Ambassadors focus only on the specific *vehicle* they're driving. They have to figure out a way to tie the vehicle *to your dealership*, not just to Toyota as the umbrella brand. It's also important that the Brand Ambassador uses his or her own voice and style in their posts. Otherwise, it looks like a scripted commercial, and the impact is nowhere near as high.

Occasionally, even the best plans go a bit sideways. We brought on an influencer once who had a huge Austin-based following and was a very, shall we say, "free person." She posted a photo hugging a tree while wearing a thong. It was—how can I say this tactfully—way off-brand. While she was a lovely person, we quickly recognized that we didn't want our brand associated with inappropriate content. We wanted our influencers to have values that are similar to the dealership's values because, when they do, it's more likely that *their* followers will be our ideal customers. Funny is fine; wearing a thong while hugging a tree? Not so much.

Your customers themselves can organically become Brand Ambassadors and promoters as well. You'll likely discover that satisfied customers will spread the word about your dealership all on their own! We gave our customers referral cards, and I know exactly how many people a specific customer sent our way. If they sent us one customer, they received a certain referral bonus. If they sent another, that bonus went up. We had some customers who went through three or four of those referral cards. They organically became some of the top advocates of our brand.

## STORYTELLING

Another effective approach to branding your dealership is incorporating storytelling. Storytelling is a timeless approach that all major brands in all industries use to grab consumers' attention. When making a buying decision, customers tend to be influenced by their emotions, which are triggered by stories. Once you're able to understand the emotions of your audience, it'll be easier for you to come up with a specific and impactful marketing plan that incorporates storytelling.

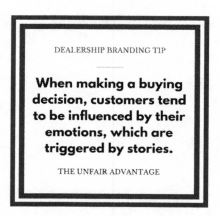

DEALERSHIP BRANDING TIP

**When making a buying decision, customers tend to be influenced by their emotions, which are triggered by stories.**

THE UNFAIR ADVANTAGE

A powerful story can captivate customers' emotions in a way that influences them to take the next step with your company. Although it's not easy to write a creative brand story, the rewards are worth the effort. The more strongly customers are able to relate to the story, the stronger the bond that can be established between your dealership and those customers. Sometimes, we used our influencers to tell stories for us. For example, one of our Brand Ambassadors posted a quick video of her in one of our cars with her girlfriends. They were singing and talking about what a great day it was. They made sure to place our logo on the post. It was a lifestyle post wherein they were having a great time in a Toyota vehicle *from our dealership*. This approach subconsciously communicated that, when you're in a Toyota, you're having fun with your friends. Or, when you want to have fun with your friends, you can do so in a Toyota (from our dealership, of course!).

Part of branding through storytelling is also demonstrating how your brand impacts society and the community. If you deal in hybrid cars, for example, you can work to show customers the importance of their role in controlling environmental pollution. Another example is, perhaps a vehicle isn't technically a hybrid, but it's fuel-efficient. We had a number of vehicles on our lot at all times that were fuel-efficient, which is a big plus when you're selling fuel efficiency.

When a customer visits a showroom to purchase a vehicle, they tend to focus on a vehicle's features and functions. They may ask for a test drive and make a final decision once they're satisfied with a vehicle's quality. In today's world of social media, specifications of a car are still important, however the outward appearance of a vehicle has become a more crucial factor than any other when it comes to making the emotional connection that causes a customer say, "That's the car I want."

The beauty of this reality is that, when you login to your account on Facebook, Instagram, or any other social network, you may see an image of a friend posing with his newly purchased vehicle. In all likelihood, if someone is choosing to show a picture of his or her new vehicle, they're proud of it. It's shiny and free of major dents, rust, or hail damage. Showing a vehicle with faded paint and dents on the body impacts the poster's reputation—and we all know one's quality of life is exactly the way it's displayed on social media, right? People are prone to exaggerate toward their most happy, successful self. Therefore, most customers who are going to share posts of their new car (or shoes or house) will do so when that item is impressive in appearance. So the fear that someone will post a picture of their car, tag your dealership, and have a negative effect on your brand is not a necessary one to have.

I have a friend who will never buy a Nissan. She's never had a bad personal experience with Nissan nor does she know anyone who has. When she was in college, in fact, she fell in love with the look of the Nissan Pathfinder. While she was home for winter break, she mentioned to her dad (who is not a car expert) that she really liked the Pathfinder. His response was, "Don't ever buy a Nissan." When she asked why, he responded, "They're always rusted out on the side of the road." She's never seen a rusted-out Nissan on the side of the road—except in her mind. To this day, anytime she sees a Nissan or hears about Nissan as a brand—that's all she can think about, so she claims she'll never buy one. That's the story that's cemented in her brain when it comes to Nissan.

Unfortunately, we can't control the ideas others put into our heads about brands or products based on their opinions or experiences. However, if we acknowledge that we have a huge opportunity to control that narrative with positive messages, stories, and experiences, we lessen the likelihood that one person's opinion can have this strong of a long-term effect!

A critical component of effective storytelling is being sure that you're tying the story back to your brand's mission and values. Therefore, don't tell a story or position your dealership in a certain way that's out of line with your dealership's core mission and values simply because you think it might get you 15 minutes of internet fame. The long-term effect of this approach is not what you want, trust me.

You can identify what kind of stories will best resonate with your market by paying attention *to* your market. What's important to them? What are their interests? What kinds of activities does their lifestyle include? Given that Charles Maund Toyota is based in Austin, many of their customers are avid University of Texas fans and/or quite loyal to Austin as an incredible city in which to live and work. So when they feature local businesses, the university, or local residents in their stories, those stories are well-received.

They know that customers looking for a minivan or other family vehicle are concerned with vehicle safety, so they tell stories around families who want to love driving their vehicles while feeling confident that their family is as safe as can be in the event of an accident. They know that their customers are often saving for kids' college funds or family trips, so they base their stories on how customers can enjoy a luxurious vehicle while saving money on both the vehicle itself as well as gas costs with more eco-friendly vehicles.

Their customers are committed to the local businesses and the Austin scene as whole, so they make sure to be clear through their stories that they give back to and are active within the community.

**WHY BUY?**

An often overlooked way to brand your dealership is through your website content. Charles Maund Toyota's website is robust, to say the least. There is little that one can't learn, explore, or schedule from their site.

Their location and phone numbers (both local and toll-free) are clearly visible. The direct phone number for their service department is also clearly visible. Visitors can access specials and rebates, new inventory, and pre-owned inventory as well as obtain financing, book service appointments, and learn about fleet sales all from the home page of the website.

They make it completely clear that, if you purchase your

vehicle from them, you'll get roadside assistance and no-cost service included, and that the dealership has an Express Maintenance option for customers who are short on time. The bottom line is that the impression a visitor to the website is left with is that Charles Maund Toyota is all about service. It gives customers the confidence that if they purchase their vehicle from them, they will be well taken care of even after they drive away in their new car. This is what keeps customers coming back to and referring the dealership year after year, making it the number one dealership in Austin.

# HUMANIZE THE DEALERSHIP

W e've established the importance of branding the dealership. The next approach that most talk about is providing value to customers. But before we dive into that, there's a second key principle we must address: humanizing the dealership. It's a crucial principle, and the point of it is simple: let customers know that real people work there.

Statistics confirm that many people claim that they'd rather be burned alive than talk to a car salesman. When I first heard that, I almost couldn't believe it. I understand that buying a car isn't on the top of most people's Fun Things to Do This Weekend list, but to rather be burned alive? That was shocking. This is exactly why humanizing the dealership is so important. It shows customers that real people work there. The other side of that coin is that customers are also real people, and they will have real experiences, reactions and opinions—both positive and negative.

The fact is, people have historically had some really bad experiences purchasing vehicles, and that's unfortunate. Charles Maund Toyota loves their customers, both long-term and brand new, and while they know they won't be able to please everyone, it's their aim to provide everyone who walks through their doors with an incredible experience from start to finish, regardless of whether or not they leave with keys to a new vehicle.

Progressive Insurance is a great example of a company that knows how to solidly humanize a brand. Progressive is known for providing fantastic service to their customers, but they're also known for Flo, their brand spokesperson. They're so well-known for her, in fact, that somewhat recently she made an appearance at various brick-and-mortar Progressive offices, and people absolutely flocked to meet the brand behind the brand. People may recognize that they aren't going to meet Flo herself when they go into a Progressive store, but they hope (and, frankly, assume) that whomever they come into contact with will have that same friendly vibe. And Progressive hopes that many of them will leave the store with new or updated insurance policies.

Another great example is Nordstrom. Customers have long valued the department store for its no-questions-asked return policy. Any item can be returned for any reason, with or without a receipt, at any time. Combine that with the restaurant and piano player available in most locations, and people tend to view and remember the shopping experience at Nordstrom as one that is extremely pleasant.

## HANDLING BAD REVIEWS

Part of humanizing the dealership is, believe it or not, replying to online reviews—even if they're negative! When someone posts a positive review, it's important to reply, thank them, and communicate how glad you are that they enjoyed their experience. Also, don't forget to share this review on your social profile and dealership's website. When a customer shares positive feedback, other social media users may be influenced to purchase a vehicle from your dealership, knowing that you sell quality vehicles and offer great customer service.

Recognize that, because people are people, they will write

bad reviews. A brand's reputation depends heavily on customer reviews, and the fact of the matter is, some customers may try to take advantage of this situation by making a false claim about an incident in order to hamper your reputation or encourage you to give them something for free simply to save the dealership from bad press.

Yelp occasionally made our dealership look like the devil incarnate. When someone wrote a bad review on this site, we tried to reach out to make the situation right, but you just can't please some people. When replying to unhappy customers, handle the conversation carefully. In the end, what they say and how they say it reflects upon them. How *you* respond reflects upon the dealership! If the review is negative, apologize for the customer's poor experience. Encourage them to contact you directly so that you can discuss it further and make it right. Help them believe that the next time they'll enjoy a far better experience. Don't, however, get into a long debate via a comment thread. This rarely, if ever, ends well. Simply encourage the customer to contact you directly via phone so that you can discuss the situation further. This is part of letting them know that there is a human being on the other end of a less-than-great transaction who wants to help make things better. It humanizes your dealership *and* contributes to your brand's reputation.

Admittedly, some situations are simply impossible to make right. One Sunday, I took the time to drive to a customer's house. The dealership was closed that day, and she needed a paper plate but didn't have a printer. I physically printed out the paper plate for her and affixed it to her car. A year later, she came into the dealership for an oil change, and while the work was being done on her car, she stated that I'd promised her three years' worth of free oil changes. I politely communicated that I hadn't promised that, and that I had it in writing that I'd promised two free oil changes (which she'd already used). She threatened to write a bad review online if I didn't give her the three years' worth of free oil changes. I responded that it was unfortunate that she was choosing to go in that direction.

Clearly still unsatisfied, she proceeded to inform me that she wasn't going to pay for the oil change she was currently receiving. I didn't now what else to do but say, "I appreciate that you came here for your service. I'm going to go ahead and cover this oil change, but I'm going to ask that in the future you visit another dealership for service." This was the first time in my entire career that I've asked a customer to go to another dealership. The situation was simply too over-the-top, and I was sure that it was only the tip of the iceberg in terms of our inability to make this particular customer happy. I believe I can turn any customer into a happy customer, but this one was a bit of a lost cause. My customer relations manager, Lauren, said to me afterward, "Chris, I don't know how you even composed yourself!" because the customer was actually yelling at me the entire time.

She indeed posted a bad review on Yelp later that day, and because viewers of her review had only her side of the story, our dealership looked bad. That's simply an aspect of humanizing the dealership over which you don't have control, and it contributes to public perception of your *brand* in a way you can't control. At some point, however, you have to simply focus on what you *are* doing right and provide as much value to your other customers every single day as you can.

As you're no doubt aware, negative social media posts go viral in a heartbeat. We once had a disgruntled customer post in a group of 10,000 people that our dealership sold her husband a warranty he didn't need. After a phone call explaining to the customer (her husband) that we had him on video saying "Yes" to the warranty purchase (legally), he acknowledged that he hadn't given his wife this piece of information. Afterward, she took the review down. However, the "damage" was already done to a degree because a large number of people in that group had seen her post and formed an opinion of our dealership based on it. If they'd never before heard of or dealt with us and this was their first impression, it wasn't a good one.

If you fail to provide satisfactory service to a customer and they leave negative feedback directly on your social media page, it can quickly tarnish your reputation. This review will convince potential customers that they should buy their next vehicle from another dealership—one that delivers better customer service.

In all cases of negative reviews, be human in your response. There is a fine line between when (and to what degree) to get involved and when it's best to wish the keyboard warriors well and get back to doing what you do best. Also important to note: positive reviews are filtered out from some review sites if your company isn't paying for their service. Many brands aren't aware of this, and most customers don't recognize that some review services are biased in this way toward companies who are compensating them to filter out bad reviews and push positive reviews to the top.

## CREATE COMMON BONDS

People identify with people who look like them. This is a key reason why the American Girl franchise is so successful. Little girls (and boys) are able to purchase a doll that resembles them down to their freckles, red hair, and glasses. Charles Maund Toyota employs a diverse group of talent, and understanding this aspect of human psychology has allowed them to intentionally feature that diversity in their promotional campaigns. They may feature an image of an Asian employee when they're targeting an Asian demographic with an ad, or showcase that they have bilingual salespeople to ease the minds of those customers who are more comfortable speaking Spanish. They want their customers to feel comfortable visiting the dealership, and if they're confident that they'll feel like they're in an inclusive environment, they're far more likely to stop in.

Another frequently used tactic we employed was posting

videos with car buying tips and featuring employees in those videos. That way, not only could customers identify with the dealership employees' physical attributes, they could "meet" them and see that they are real people. This approach created a far more personal buying experience—the customer felt like he knew the person from whom he was considering purchasing a vehicle.

Social media advertising is inexpensive enough that you can easily and cost-effectively target target segments of the population. While this may sound a bit controversial, the fact is that when companies create a commercial to speak directly to the African-American population through BET, they typically have African-American individuals in that ad. If an ad for an American-made product is featured on Telemundo, the ad will be in Spanish. If I'm in Paris and I want to buy a car, and I know (because of advertising) that a specific car dealership in Paris has an English-speaking salesperson, I'm going to feel more comfortable walking into that dealership. It's not about calling out a demographic, it's about speaking directly *to* them and providing phenomenal service to them and their unique needs. It's important to connect with people and let them know that they'll feel comfortable coming to your dealership because they're not going to be the only African-American or Spanish-speaker or woman there.

There is a phenomenal salesperson from Venezuela at Charles Maund. Believe it or not, there are lots of Venezuelans living in Austin. I've never seen a salesperson reach a community as effectively as he has. Almost every customer he sells to is from that community. From his sales, we can target not only his customer base through ads but also his customers' friends. I've never signed as many referral checks as I've signed to his customers.

At Charles Maund, I had an employee and great friend named Miguel Vega-Centeno. He created a Facebook group for Spanish speaking people in Austin. He ended up growing the group to over 126,000 people, and he lives off of customer referrals only at that one dealership. What's unique about his situation is that his family was deported, and he only gets to see them for a week at a time every other month. Because he was able to so effectively get his customers working for him, his been able to support two households on his earnings from one position.

We once made a video featuring one of our salespeople who happen to be Asian. We then targeted that ad to every individual of Asian descent in the general area who we'd pre-qualified as an "intender"—someone who had shown interest in purchasing a Toyota vehicle by applying for a loan at an Austin-based dealership. The way we determine that is through purchasing car loan application data from Oracle, Experian, and Equifax. This particular salesperson consistently sells more cars since enacting this approach.

**GET COMFORTABLE WITH VIDEO**

When salespeople say they aren't comfortable making videos, I get it. I can't tell you how uncomfortable I am making videos. Right before I hit *Share*, I think "Ohmigosh, do I really want to do this?" I start talking myself out of it, and then I turn around and talk myself back up, and then I hit *Share*. I do these videos completely on-the-fly. I don't spend hours on end scripting them or re-recording over errors. I know what I'm going to talk about ahead of time, but on-the-fly comes off as far more genuine. After I record a video, I send it to someone to do some minor editing and put some graphics on, but that's it.

I know at a high level at the beginning of each week what topics I want to talk about, and then I think through a variety of ways to approach that particular topic in short bursts. Two- or three-minute videos are best in this industry; they hold people's attention. The last thing you want is for a customer to feel like a video from your dealership is never going to end and clicking out of it. That's the last thing they remember about your dealership. Not, "Oh, another great tip from Charles Maund" but "Oh geez, it's them again."

Many dealerships are hesitant to put their employees on video. They're afraid of losing control of the brand. I truly believe this fear is unfounded and a mistake. It's critical to have people working at your dealership who you're proud to employ. And if you're proud to employ them, why not share them!

## SALESPERSON BRANDING

It's so important for the the salespeople to brand *themselves* through social media as well. Many dealerships are resistant to this idea because they fear that if the salesperson quits, he'll take his customers with him. The fact of the matter is, if he quits, he's going to do that anyway. You might as well give him the best tools to sell more cars and be sure that you're treating them well. If they're being treated well and making good money, they won't want to go anywhere else!

When I sold cars, I branded myself as a salesperson *specifically* at the dealership. And guess what? Had I left to work at another dealership, all of my customers would have come to see me wherever I went, regardless of what brand of car I was selling because of the way I took care of them! I didn't leave to sell cars at another dealership. I left to run The AutoMiner, the database mining solution I built to solve the problems I struggled with when I was trying to efficiently and effectively market our dealership, which is having an incredible effect on the industry. More on that shortly.

When I went back to selling cars, Facebook existed, but it wasn't as effective was it is today. There weren't as many people using it as there are at this point in time. I used to mail flyers to my clients through the postal service, but today a salesperson could create a professional Facebook page in order to boost posts or use their personal profile in order to engage with and provide value to his or her community. There are so many Facebook groups in each city that salespeople can become a member of, not to mention churches, your kid's school, and other community-based groups where you can easily engage with community members. It can be hard to reach that number of people face-to-face, but with Facebook and other social media platforms, you can participate in community functions and events without actually being there physically.

You can't boost posts from a personal profile, and technically, according to current Facebook rules, you're not supposed to be doing business from your personal profile. But providing value and genuinely interacting is not the same as doing business. Be wary of providing links in the body of your posts, and ask yourself, "What value am I providing through this post?" As long as you can answer that question, you're probably okay.

There are so many people in my neighborhood group on Facebook, and it's easy to begin having a non-sales-focused conversation in the group and become involved in what people are posting. You're saying to people, "I live in your neighborhood. I'm real. And I'd love to help!" This approach takes far less time than going door-to-door, and it's never before been a possibility at the scale that it is today. People can see who you are before they ever visit a dealership.

You cannot be like an animal going after clients, however, which unfortunately happens all the time on social media. People are quick to constantly post links and send unsolicited invitations via private message for a consultation. It's nonsense. My approach is to ask myself, *How can I provide value here?* In most cases, the answer to that is simple: answer the question that's been asked!

HUMANIZE THE DEALERSHIP

## When posting to social media, ask yourself, "How can I provide value?"

THE UNFAIR ADVANTAGE

Salespeople are so focused on getting the sale that they don't build basic camaraderie first. People buy from people they like, and this is why it's so effective to become part of relevant groups, be yourself, and make some new friends. You have to find common ground. You have to make a "five-minute friend." If they trust you and you take care of them, they're more than likely going to consider you when they need whatever it is that you sell. The end game isn't *How am I going make money off this person?* Ultimately, making money will be the result of treating someone right even when they don't need anything from you. As long as you treat them right, build value in the product, and show them the right information, you will likely sell them a car at some point—and, in turn, make money.

When you're participating in a Facebook group, even if it's a huge group, if you start to consistently engage with others, people begin to know who you are and what you do. It requires a good bit of work, yes, but it's a far more efficient approach overall. It's just about treating people right and making connections. I had a meeting this morning I'm not sure I ever would have been able to get had the intermediary not been my boss back in 2005. We've kept in contact over the years through social media, and he just moved up a lot further in the food chain than I did. But now here we are working on a deal together. Had I not met him back then and made the effort to keep the relationship going because I genuinely like him, who knows how I would have been able to make this deal?

Additionally, don't forget the fact that if you provide value to someone who isn't your customer, maybe their aunt or best friend or next-door neighbor *is* your customer, and because you provided value, you'll be recommended.

If dealerships end up with a salesperson who is branding themselves (and, therefore, the dealership) in a poor way, they can simply let that person know that they aren't going to support them. Meaning, they aren't going to share their posts. Meaning, they aren't going to help leverage them and bring more customers to that salesperson specifically. I had a salesperson once who cussed all the time. I just said, "I'm not going to associate the dealership brand with that." I wasn't willing to promote him as a Brand Ambassador and salesperson. Some companies can get away with being more outspoken because it's who they are as a brand, but you have to be really aware of who you represent and who your brand is at its core so that your posts are inline with brand values.

My wife was on the NextDoor app several months ago, and there was a realtor who had done a great job of branding himself as the realtor for our neighborhood. So when it came time to sell our house, she said, "Why don't you talk to that guy?" I reached out to him, and as it turned out, he already had a buyer who was interested in my house. I didn't even have to officially list it! This is the aspect of social media people don't make the most of—the number of people you can reach while saving an incredible amount of time.

The viral nature (both positive and negative) of social media is a great testament to why it's so important to handle situations and people in a way you're proud of as a human being. You just never know when they might be able to be of value down the line, or vice versa. If you handle a deal that doesn't go through or a supervisor you don't particularly care for in a bad way, and an opportunity arises later that you're afraid to approach because of the way things ended between you previously, it's an unfortunately lost opportunity.

## CUSTOMER-FOCUSED EVENTS

Charles Maund loves to get to know their customers better—even after they've made a purchase—and so they host specific events in order to do so. One event that's held once each quarter is a truck event. Toyota offers a number of 4-wheel drive vehicles, and many owners wonder where they can even go off-roading in Austin. They are also rarely aware of all that their truck can do (because they aren't off-roading!). Everyone who has purchased a truck or 4-wheel drive vehicle from the dealership is invited. The dealership arrives with food and everyone has e a fantastic time.

It's commonplace for dealerships to sponsor local events. In many cases, they simply send a banner advertising the dealership to be displayed during the event. We took it a step further and actually *showed up* at the events! We attended a number of events in support of the Chamber of Commerce, the Hispanic Chamber of Commerce, and charities the dealership sponsors. It's a great opportunity not only to more personally support the organizations you care about but also meet attendees in person, put a face (or two) with your brand, and learn from one-on-one conversations how you might be able to help people in the market for a new vehicle.

The dealership also hosts clinics for new owners. Customers can come in and learn how to use their vehicle—they get to glean all the little nuances they may not have figured out yet like cruise control or automatic headlights. The previous Internet Director hosted Women Shop Wednesdays, where businesses that cater to women would come in and setup a table or provide complimentary chair massages. It was almost like there was a little boutique inside the showroom. Just recently, Lisa

Copeland, who owned the number one Fiat dealership in the country, hosted 300 or so women at the dealership and did a presentation to raise awareness for breast cancer.

We've had networking events where we invited other industry professionals (in any industry, not just the automotive industry) to come in for breakfast and get to know other local business owners or professionals. Those events are great for new salespeople as well because they teach them how to move around and talk to new people. All these kinds of events bring more attention to a dealership. Dealerships doing something similar could absolutely advertise such events via Facebook ads and ask people to RSVP.

# PROVIDE VALUE TO CUSTOMERS AND COMMUNITY

N ow that we've discussed the importance of both branding and humanizing the dealership, let's talk about the many ways to provide incredible value to both current and new customers—the kind of value they won't soon forget.

PROVIDE VALUE

**The connection and rapport you build with customers is more critical than you can even imagine.**

THE UNFAIR ADVANTAGE

It's truly the lynchpin of the entire marketing process. How well you retain your customers is what will determine the degree of long-term growth you experience.

At Charles Maund Toyota, there are approximately 120,000 customers in the main database. The average dealer has 10,000 to 30,000 customers in their database, and more rural dealers have 2,000-5,000 customers in their database. When dealerships communicate that they aren't making a strong effort to stay in touch with past customers, I'm instantly confused. That's an awful lot of people to "ignore" simply because the process of meeting with them and possibly selling them a vehicle has ended (for now).

It's not enough to provide customers with value at time-of-service alone; two years down the road, the customer will have forgotten specifically who they worked with at your dealership (or forgotten about your dealership altogether in light of competing dealerships in the area who grab their attention daily via their own digital marketing strategy!). Additionally, there are many opportunities to provide service to customers in between car purchases and many dealerships neglect these opportunities.

Most dealerships are focused primarily on acquiring new customers rather than continuing to serve current customers. This is where the concept of branding comes back into play. Your brand has to be the obvious choice when someone needs or wants a new car. But your dealership also has to be the obvious choice when customers need service on their car—or when someone the brand of vehicle your dealership specializes in moves in to the area and needs a service group or is unhappy with their dealership's service team and ready to try someone new. Your existing customers are the most important asset your company has. You need to retain them in order for your dealership to flourish.

## DIRECT MAIL

While direct mail may be seen as an "old school" method of advertising, based on the volume of advertisements landing in my own mailbox everyday, it's clearly alive and doing (very) well.

In the car dealership industry, direct mail continues to be a successful way not only to keep your brand in front of current customers but also to provide them with value they don't expect. While it sometimes seems archaic, snail mail is still quite effective in some niches. For example, I buy all my suits at Brooks Brothers. They recently sent me a little pot of honey. I know it's just one of their little marketing ploys, but it still felt pretty nice to receive it, and my immediate thought was, "Do I need a new suit?"

*\*Sidenote: Be sure to know your city's and state's rules and regulations when it comes to sending direct mail. They change frequently, and getting a penalty for inadvertently breaking the law is not only a headache, it's expensive.*

I used to send a postcard to customers every month with a photo of an amazing dessert along with the recipe for that dessert. My photo was front and center as well (in this case, customers would remember me as their salesperson as well as the dealership name). The copy on the postcard would read, "I like car buyers like you, and I'll gladly send you $100 for any referral you send my way! In the meantime, enjoy this great dessert!" People would come into the dealership and say, "Chris, I've been making your recipes!" I'll admit, that kind of shocked me. I didn't want to send them a postcard that seemed to only be about what *they* could do for *us* (give us referrals); I also wanted to provide value to *them* (in the form of a great recipe). I just had no idea how much they'd be appreciated! Customers didn't simply throw out the postcard because they wanted to check out the recipe. Sometimes, they kept that recipe in a drawer or on their refrigerator, which provided a constant reminder of our dealership.

Realtors do this all the time with calendars, emails detailing local weekend activities, and refrigerator magnets with a place to write important emergency numbers (right underneath their brand's logo and phone number, of course). With this approach,

I was in front of customers every single month. While realtors have to be in front of customers forever because people don't necessarily buy new houses every single year, the length of time between vehicle purchases is rarely that long.

## VOICEMAIL MARKETING

Voicemail marketing is also a critical way to stay in touch with customers and provide value at the same time. I had a customer who bought a car from me about 12 months ago at an 18% interest rate. He made his payments on time and so his credit improved. I left him a voicemail, letting him know that I had an opportunity to help him lower his payment and get into a new vehicle at the same time. He called back shortly thereafter, and I got him from an 18% to a 4% interest rate on a brand new vehicle. There were many months where spending $1,000 on direct voicemail marketing netted 30 additional sales for us.

There are several critical touch-points in the buying cycle when a dealership can successfully engage a customer. Customers are usually changing their vehicle every two to three years, but beyond that there are certain data sets that you can utilize to compel them to come in earlier.

## SERVICE SERVICE SERVICE

You likely already know that a dealership cannot sustain itself by selling cars alone. Margins are continuing to shrink, and the fact is, money is made in service. This is precisely why I developed The AutoMiner three years ago. I recognized that we could reduce our marketing costs *and* have a better way to re-market to our previous clients in far less time and with almost no manpower.

Whether or not you use a software like The AutoMiner, it's crucial to engage customers and stay in touch with them. Customers prefer dealing with a business that knows their needs and is ready to address any issues they may face, now or in the future.

One of the biggest problems dealerships have is that once a car is out of factory warranty, customers start going to third party services such as Jiffy Lube to have maintenance work done. They often don't recognize that dealerships have the brand-specific knowledge and technology to properly service their vehicles, whereas third-party solutions don't. They defect and go to, for example, Jiffy Lube for a $19.99 oil change. Short term, saving a few dollars can be appealing. Long term, you get what you pay for.

The reason Jiffy Lube and similar companies came around is that dealerships were greatly messing up in this area. The first thing I recommend to dealers is to focus on their existing owner base and take care of their customers to ensure that they'll keep coming back. One of the groups that dealerships neglect or outright forget about is their service tribe, which is made up of everyone who's purchased a car from them as well as anyone in the area who owns their brand of vehicle. By focusing on that part of their business, they can get customers back in between car purchases. And guess what? When you're already servicing these customers, chances are high that you can easily sell them another car when the time comes, or gain a referral based on how well you treated them at time of service.

A friend of mine always took her car to Jiffy Lube for oil changes and tire rotations. When she bought her Camry, it came with Toyota's 2-year care plan whereby all standard service appointments in the first two years are completely covered when you get your car serviced at a Toyota dealership. What customer wouldn't take advantage of this? It saves them at least $25 every time they need to have their oil changed!

If the brand of vehicle your dealership sells doesn't offer this kind of a service at the uppermost level, you can still work it in to your dealership's offerings, either as an add-on when a customer purchases a car or as a service that your dealership offers (just be sure to work the cost in somewhere). You're providing great service up front as well as ensuring that you get to stay in front of your customers every few months for as long as they own that vehicle. It's a win-win situation! Audi and BMW have 4-year/50,000 mile service coverage plans. You can come up with a plan that works for your dealership, but it's most certainly a value to your customers and a benefit to your dealership that I highly recommend you consider.

When a customer doesn't have to worry about paying for their service, they're more likely to get their service completed on time, ensuring that their car is properly cared for (so that if/when they trade it in, you've got fewer issues to repair before re-selling it). When customers go to a third-party automotive service establishment, they often complain that they don't have the confidence that what the establishment is saying is wrong with their car is really wrong. They don't know if they are simply being up-sold based on their lack of knowledge.

I asked my friend about her experience taking her Camry to her local Toyota dealership for service because I know this is the first time she's had a routine service plan included with a vehicle purchase. She commented that the service she receives is phenomenal. When she pulls into the service lane, they immediately approach. They're expecting her, and they know why she's there. While she's waiting, she's often looking at other vehicles in the showroom! Or, she's doing work in their nicely appointed waiting room, complete with flat-screen TV, cold bottled water, and coffee. She doesn't dread having to sit in the dealership for 30-60 minutes while they service her car the way you might at a cold, dingy, third-party establishment.

Another benefit I hadn't even thought about is that she has begun to develop a rapport with the service staff. The same individuals are there each time, and so when it comes time to purchase a new vehicle, while she recognizes that the service staff isn't on the sales floor, the generally great brand she's come to trust at that dealership will compel her to look there first.

Most dealerships are really missing a huge opportunity if they aren't taking care of the service portion of their business in order to grow their sales. More than anything else, dealerships simply aren't proactive enough in their service departments. Some do a great job with it, but with unemployment as low as it is, it could be so much better in most cases. During the financial crisis of 2008, unemployment got up to 11% or 12%, so the fact that it's under 4% right now is pretty huge. Who knows when the next bust will happen (I predict it will be in 2020 or 2021), but you have to be prepared for it regardless. Part of a solid retention plan is ensuring that if your sales are going to decrease, you're ready to shift your focus to servicing customers. You have to make sure you have processes in place so that you can survive any downturn and then continue marketing to those customers when the market turns around again (because it always does).

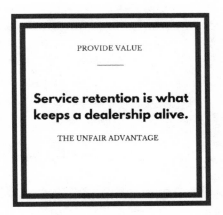

PROVIDE VALUE

**Service retention is what keeps a dealership alive.**

THE UNFAIR ADVANTAGE

Service retention is what keeps a dealership alive. It's easy to go after the low-hanging fruit, but how can you go after *all* of the fruit. Do you have the correct processes in place to go after the fruit at the top of the tree? If you have a BDC (Business Development Center), that group is going for the top of the tree. But they might not be doing it as efficiently as they could be. The AutoMiner's automated process goes after *all* the fruit while increasing a dealership's efficiency and reducing their costs. Our results prove this. We've taken segments to which it would take a BDC an entire month to make calls and knocked them out in an hour or two, all while increasing the number of appointments made as well as the number of appointments to which customers show up via SMS reminders.

If your service drive is like Charles Maund's, it's jam-packed in the morning, but by afternoon there's not much going on out there. I wondered how we could optimize the service drive's daily schedule and fill it with customers from morning until end of day. The AutoMiner plugs into your DMS and automates appointment scheduling and appointment reminders. It then syncs with whatever scheduling service you use. It removes the human component entirely. Not only do you schedule more appointments and service more customers, you don't have to pay employee salaries or benefits, and you don't have to worry about scheduling assistants calling in sick. The AutoMiner is always on time, and it runs 24 hours a day, 7 days a week.

The reality of a downturn or complete recession is undeniable, and you have to be prepared. I distinctly remember a time when I was on the floor selling and simultaneously watching the dealer one parking lot over door shut their doors. I watched entire groups go out of business. I also remember what it was like seeing three manufacturers ask Congress for a bailout. In these moments, you have to create your own economy. You need to be setup now in order to ensure that you can survive and even thrive in the next recession.

The alternative to closing your dealership during a recession is figuring out ways to maintain your customers and keep your employees happy (by not having to cut salaries and benefits). How do you capture and retain your clients, and what happens when it all hits the fan? Do you have a plan and a process to continue serving clients? At some point, there is going to be another catastrophe. Are you prepared? Do you have the right processes in place to serve your clients and stay solvent?

**"In a down market the best do good, and in an up market the best do great."**

Right now, Charles Maund uses SMS technology strictly for service reminders. There is a widget on their website that helps a customer automatically schedule his or her service appointment right from the website. If you have to rely on employees to take these calls and schedule these appointments, you're paying an employee and that person is only working during normal business hours. The Artificial Intelligence within The AutoMiner helps tremendously with the tedious work that was, until now, associated with service scheduling. The website widget is operational 24 hours a day, 7 days a week to schedule appointments. It then sends out SMS notifications at different mileage intervals in order to remind customers that it's time to come back in for a regular maintenance checkup. It's not enough for a customer to simply see the maintenance light light up on their dash. We have to make the extra effort to get them in.

BDC agents will make 6,000-7,000 phone calls a month on average, but The AutoMiner can manage that amount of traffic in an hour. Most dealerships spend $5,000-$10,000 per quarter to send out snail mail with oil change coupons. Through The AutoMiner, we can generate several thousand text messages a month and a couple hundred appointments automatically. When a customer schedules a service appointment, our system knows exactly who they are (if they've been here before) and what service they are due for. The Artificial Intelligence component will actually schedule the appointment for them and find out where to send the reminders. There is no human interaction required at all! And because this isn't where customers want human interaction, it's an area where dealerships can effectively cut costs and re-direct man hours to sales and retention.

Customers are also able to text a dealership's ChatBot system if they need to schedule service or make an inquiry. Through Facebook messenger, a dealership's Artificial Intelligence recognizes who the customer is, schedules his appointment, and puts it into the system within a minute or two. There is no employee interaction at all. These are the incredible valuable approaches that dealerships are overlooking. I lost two service advisors last year. There were normally eight of them, but we lost two. It didn't even have that great of an affect on us because of these automated process.

## BE WHERE YOUR CUSTOMERS ARE

When developing your marketing strategy, not only should you take into account the current needs and lifestyles of your customer base, you should also focus on where they may be heading in the future.

One of the best ways to determine where your customers are is to observe their behavior when they're in the dealership, especially when they're there for service on their vehicle. They're likely on their phones or tablets. If you have a TV on, they may be choosing to watch that instead. If you can, identify which devices they're on and what they're doing on them. These people are already your customers, so observing their actual behavior is the most authentic way to assess those behaviors and the way they choose to consume information.

Marketing teams tend to stick to approaches that have worked in the past. It's what they're comfortable with. However, you must always be on the lookout for new and different approaches and stay aware of where people's attention is. If a strong contingency of your target demographic suddenly becomes interested in Music.ly for example, you'll meed to be ready to create and maintain a brand presence there.

Charles Maund is nearby the University of Texas campus, and they know that many college students use Snapchat. Therefore, they use Snapchat in our marketing efforts as well. If you're in an area with an older population, perhaps that wouldn't be as effective an approach. Just two years ago, 70% of our ideal customers were using desktop computers. Now, 70% have converted to primarily mobile use. This forced us to change our strategy and the platforms on which we were executing that strategy. You simply have to know where the trend is for your audience and ensure you're there. You have to be where your customer's attention is.

I wish it were easier in our industry to identify clear customer avatars, but in many cases dealerships sell to a little bit of almost every demographic. It's hard to simply market one way because, for example, if we look at how our customers shop, the details of their approaches are quite different. You have to be aware that people with different shopping habits are still your target customers and tailor your marketing campaigns to a broad range of people and then segment down as best you can. In order to scale a particular strategy, you simply identify one that's working! We looked at the approaches of our competitors who were doing the most sales, and we went for the low-hanging fruit first. People who buy minivans generally have young kids, and we could easily target that demographic with our Facebook ads. We could target individuals who were likely expecting a baby with minivan ads as well.

Simply because we knew how much our ideal customers use Facebook, we had an incredibly robust Facebook presence. Due to the frequency of our Facebook content and ability to target specific groups, people often approached me in public and asked, "Where do I know you from?" or said, "You're the Toyota guy!" A friend of mine from another dealership has his face on a few billboards and gets the same kind of response but at 10 times the expense.

Regardless of which platform you're using, ease of contact

and full transparency are key to positively increasing brand awareness. When someone visits a brand's social media profile, they want to learn more about their services and products. Some businesses tend to hide necessary information from customers. For instance, they post the price of a product but don't mention hidden charges such as a shipping fee or taxes. The idea that you can get a customer into the dealership with a spectacular offer (leaving out the fine print) and then "win them over" once they are in the dealership is not one that typically ends successfully. If you want to succeed in the digital world and increase sales, it's important to be transparent. Inform followers about *actual* vehicle prices and refrain from hiding any facts and figures. If you deal in used vehicles, it's best to guide followers up-front when it comes to any potential problems a vehicle may have. This practice builds trust which, in turn, creates a strong brand reputation and strengthens your relationship with customers.

## QUALITY OVER QUANTITY

Many dealerships have a misconception that the more they post —specifically on Facebook, LinkedIn, and other social media sites—the more they'll be able to engage customers. This statement is true to some extent; however, if you prefer quantity over quality, your content won't keep the attention of your ideal customer base for very long.

Staying active and consistent on social media is important for communicating and engaging with your customer base, but be wary of overlooking the importance of quality content. Quality posts catch the eye of social media users and compel them to like, comment, or share. The more likes, comments, and shares a post receives, the more it will organically be shown in the feeds of your followers. Low-quality content, on the other hand, will be of little interest to followers and may actually compel them to hide your posts or unfollow you altogether, which does nothing but undermine your marketing strategy.

While posting consistently is important, posting *too* frequently is an approach that usually backfires—mostly because all of the posts are not of quality. Dealerships are simply pushing to post "at least six times per day," even if a post or two is wildly irrelevant or boring. Be sure to conduct a social media audit report and base your posting strategy on the results of that report. Among other benefits, this report will guide you on how frequently your industry should post on social media for ideal engagement.

With regard to how often to post, it's common for brands to wonder, "How often is too often? And how often isn't often enough?" Many businesses don't realize that they are, in fact, spamming their followers. When it comes to Facebook, most experts suggest posting between one and five times per day. The key to attracting and retaining followers is posting valuable information. This information can grab the attention of current followers, attract new followers, and convert both into paying customers. However, a problem arises when businesses become too sales-focused. In their attempt to sell more vehicles to more customers, they forget the importance of adding value to their customers' lives. A good rule to follow is the 80/20 principle, which suggests that you post 20% sales content and 80% entertaining and educational posts. This way, your followers won't get bored, and they'll be intrigued when you *do* have a compelling offer they can benefit from.

For Twitter, the recommendation typically is 10 to 15 posts per day. Don't overload your profiles with what are clearly automated posts or cross-posts between your social media platforms. Social media platforms are just that—social—and they are different from one another for a reason. While it's efficient, taking a post from Twitter and auto-posting it to your Facebook page often looks lazy to the follower who can see that it's a cross-post. Some platforms favor hashtags while others do not. Social media platforms aren't one-size-fits-all, and it's rarely successful to treat them as though they are because it dehumanizes the dealership. Do you see the important correlation between humanizing your dealership, properly positioning your brand, and attracting (as well as retaining) followers?

Just as over-posting on social media can be harmful, neglecting your social media accounts can produce less-than-optimal results. If a social media user visits your profile to learn more about your services, they'll likely check the date of your most recent post. If you haven't posted in months or even weeks, they'll probably visit the page of one of your competitors and end up purchasing a vehicle from them instead.

Skilled social media strategists maintain a content calendar to remind them what and when to post to avoid repetition as well as over- or under-posting. Furthermore, whenever an important social or dealership-based event occurs, they are prepared to post about it. Regular posting shows that you value your customers and are there to serve them.

## EFFECTIVE CONTENT

Your dealership will benefit from content generated by your employees as well as customer-generated content. You've likely noticed your friends sharing images of products they've purchased and showcasing their favorite brands. Similarly, when a customer buys a vehicle from your dealership, they may organically promote the company through a social media post. Asking satisfied customers to leave feedback on your business profile is a great way to create valuable customer-generated content.

Digital content often has a high impact if it goes viral. While there's no definitive way to make your content go viral, make sure that your posts are useful so that social media users are tempted to share them with others. Stay up-to-date with recent events and develop content accordingly. Use powerful infographics to make your content more noticeable and visually appealing.

Refrain from sharing the exact same content in the exact same way across all accounts, even if you're not cross-posting. It's important to create fresh content for your followers on different sites. Your Instagram followers may be more interested in images and videos of cars you sell, whereas LinkedIn followers may be interested in advancements in the automotive industry, and Facebook users may appreciate car buying and driving tips.

Be *sure* your content is proofread before it's posted. Improper grammar and spelling will detract from your brand. It will, in turn, lessen your followers' interest and your overall credibility.

It's incredibly important to be strategic about not only what you're posting but *why* you're posting it. Uber and Lyft are two prominent transportation services. In early 2017, cab drivers in the U.S. announced a strike as a protest against the new immigration laws. As a marketing tactic, Uber suspended its peak pricing, and customers were infuriated. Lyft, on the other hand, made the most of this situation by sending out a solidarity message. As a consequence, thousands of users posted against Uber and preferred traveling with Lyft. CNN recently suffered backlash from inadvertently offending viewers on social media. They started a campaign under the hashtag #AskACop, whereby anyone could question a cop who had reportedly harmed others through their authority. The heated arguments that quickly ensued forced them to take down the campaign. Don't aim to anger people or cause divisive feelings if that's not what your brand is about just because you hope the controversy will create a viral post.

It's important to think of your customers as you're creating a content strategy. Many businesses make the mistake of posting only corporate, sterile content. Your social media profile should confirm that your dealership employs real people who are interested in the likes and dislikes of its customers. When you're about to make a post, ask yourself, "Would I enjoy seeing this post on my feed? Does this provide value to me in some way?"

Post content that appeals to the preferences of your target audience in order to attract and engage them. Customer engagement is essential, so if you regularly post content but receive no comments, you need to come up with a solution. Reply to comments and engage with posts—even if it's on another feed—if it's a question you can answer or a discussion where you can provide value. Don't necessarily insert yourself into the feed of a competitor, but if there is a local business or group wherein people are asking questions to which you can provide value-added answers (not just offer them a sale opportunity), it's a great opportunity to engage them and let them know that you're there and ready to help. If a user is facing issues with your products, personally guide them toward an in-person or over-the-phone way to improve their experience. Businesses that don't focus on effective customer engagement eventually lose their customer base. Add value with useful and informative content, encourage followers to share feedback, and ask them for suggestions to improve your service.

## TIPS FOR EFFECTIVE SOCIAL MEDIA CONTENT

- Avoid posting monotonous content
- Post witty comments and humorous posts for customer engagement. However, be careful when posting humorous content. Refrain from purposely or inadvertently hurting the emotions of any specific group of people. Rude behavior or insensitive content will lead to the loss of followers and may also result in having your social media profile suspended or permanently shut down.
- Share interactive posts on your Facebook or LinkedIn groups. Your followers can give their

feedback with likes or comments. Use this information to further improve your social media strategy.

- Live videos have proven extremely effective in engaging customers. Share live messages by members of top management. This shows that your company values its customers and doesn't leave any stones unturned when it comes to providing them with a great experience.

- Live videos convey the message that your business isn't solely focused on increasing sales and generating revenue. Share inspirational content with viewers in your live content. Create memorable videos with a positive message so that customers will save the videos and share them with friends. The magic question to ask yourself is, "Are we providing value to our customers through this live video?" Do be extra careful when broadcasting a live video. Even a little carelessness can attract a lot of criticism from social media users. Use a high-quality camera so that your customers can fully enjoy the content. Whenever your company arranges an event of any sort, you can broadcast it live to your social media profile. It'll increase brand awareness and ensure that your customers stay aware of the current happenings in your company.

- Gather inspiration from other brands, but DO NOT plagiarize content. Evaluate how other brands use social media to promote their product and services and then identify innovative ways to make your own social media strategy even more uniquely fruitful.

There are a number of prominent brands that make the most of their presence on social media, and you can learn from them to promote your dealership.

Lufthansa uses a shade of gold as its primary color. If you browse through their Facebook page, you'll notice this shade of gold in almost every graphic. This color isn't present only in their promotional posts but also is a part of their conversational content. Because of this, users recognize and remember the brand with ease.

Chanel is a fashion brand that relies mainly on Instagram for promotion. They post images of recent photoshoots, fashion shows, designers, celebrities wearing their clothing, lifestyle-based ads, and sketches of their latest designs.

TD Ameritrade carried out a campaign in 2014 with the hashtag #itaddsup. As we all know, athletes have to undergo intense practice sessions before being able to compete in the Olympic Games. They compared these practice sessions with small investments and showed how these small investments can combine to create a large sum in the long run. At that time, the Winter Olympics were going on, and the brand cashed in on the hype. The campaign increased their social audience by a reported 12%.

Expedia is a travel booking website that aids travelers in reserving airline tickets, hotel rooms, rental cars, vacation packages, and cruise trips. In order to stand out from the competition, they post intriguing and fascinating images of different locations and link them to blog posts on their website. These travel images encourage social media users to visit the website and book a trip.

Important to note: sharing only your own content provides a negative impression. No doubt, the major purpose of social media marketing is to promote your own business. Posting only your own advertising content, however, will eventually lead customers to unfollow you.

Trend toward posts through which you can create engagement with consumers, and don't shy away from sharing curated content. Furthermore, you can get in touch with market influencers and create collaborative videos to cross-promote your car dealership and their personal brand.

I've seen some dealerships use comedy in their posts and ads and do a really good job. Owners and salespeople get involved in the videos. The key is not to overthink it beyond a certain point. Believe it or not, there really aren't any absolutely DON'TS as far as marketing goes. I mean, obviously stay away from politics and religion, and be sure you're aware of your audience in order to ensure that they won't take a post the wrong way. Surprisingly, many brands don't seem to understand the importance of that. Even celebrities will try to be funny but occasionally push the envelope a bit too far—take Roseanne Barr or Kathy Griffin, for example. Use common sense, but always be experimenting and willing to try new things in order to attract and engage your ideal customers.

## USE LOCATION TO YOUR ADVANTAGE

My local market is Austin, Texas, which is home to between one and two million people. While I would have loved to advertise our dealership nationally or even worldwide, it was critical that I make the most noise locally that I could because most people buying a vehicle want to purchase from someone locally. There was often a ripple effect to some of our content that landed it in the feeds of other people and gained us followers outside of Austin and even outside of Texas, and that was simply a bonus of having great, relatable, shareable content. We frequently posted content related to local sports teams such as the Texas Longhorns.

In 2017, I created a show that was aired through Facebook called Austin Spotlight, which was sponsored by Charles Maund Toyota and profiled local Austin businesses in order to create shared influence. We featured anybody who was willing to come on the show. I had a guy going around just talking to business owners, saying, "Hey, let's do this!" It was free for them to come on, and we simply chatted about how they got started and why they chose Austin as their home base. We talked about their favorite places to eat and different aspects of Austin that made them love living here.

What was great about these partnerships was that the businesses that were profiled were tagged in our posts, so when they shared that post, it provided exposure to our brand as well —and at zero cost! Other times, another featured brand paid to sponsor the post from their Facebook page, and because we were mentioned, we got automatic (and free) advertising from it. I was getting free advertisement for the dealership, and customers were coming in and talking to me all the time. The only downside was that people who came in didn't seem to want to talk to one of my sales guys. They wanted to talk to me specifically. But I did sell a lot of cars as a result!

Another effective strategy is making your content work *for* you by creating multiple pieces of smaller content from one larger piece. For example, if you make a 10-minute video, break it up into different content pieces. Perhaps you have one tip in a 30-second clip (or even a 15-second clip) and expand upon it in the text copy of the post. Or, screenshot a clip of the video and have an intriguing caption placed on it that you expand upon with a valuable post. Take a Top 10 list and break it into ten different posts; simply elaborate on each individual point in the list. Or make a quick tip video related to the point. From a longer video, take a screen shot, give it a title, and break the full video into a few smaller ones with "to be continued..." at the end. It gives the user something to look forward to. The key is to be willing to try different approaches on different platforms to see what's working.

## COMMUNITY INVOLVEMENT

Charles Maund Toyota believes that the worth of a business is greatly determined by its goodwill. It's important for them to give back to local organizations that are doing good things in and for their community while letting the community know that they care about them. They partner with SafePlace, an organization that supports battered women. They also regularly support an organization that supports troubled youth as well as the Cystic Fibrosis organization. One of the owner's daughters had Cystic Fibrosis, and supporting this cause is near and dear to him.

We promote our support and attendance of certain charitable events to show our intent to raise money for that organization. Our customers are often looking for a great cause to donate to, and they want to show that they support these causes because it's indicative of who they are as a dealership. Employees are encouraged to propose new organizations or causes to support based on their own experiences. Supporting causes that your employees are passionate about is a great way to show them that you care. It's a great way to humanize the dealership for your employees, which—when combined with a great incentive and benefits package—only enhances their loyalty and performance.

# KNOW WHO'S IN CHARGE

One of the first questions I ask dealerships when talking to them about their marketing challenges is, "Who's running the show?" The two answers that make me the most nervous are, "We hired an agency to do it all" and "We have someone in our marketing department who takes care of it."

An effective, scalable marketing campaign requires a lot of consistent work. Dealerships often rely on just one marketing guy. You can't stay competitive in today's world without a solid strategy for every area of your marketing playbook. Having a well-thought-through, effective strategy is what makes the difference between selling a 100-150 cars per month and selling 300-400 cars per month.

When I stopped working at Charles Maund Toyota as their general sales manager, they had two agencies they were working with. One worked specifically with Facebook, Instagram, LinkedIn, YouTube, and Google ads; the other worked with TV and radio.

KNOW WHO'S IN CHARGE

**In order to run a successful, scalable marketing operation, you'll need to hire experts from the outside and designate managers from within to be in charge of different areas of your efforts.**

THE UNFAIR ADVANTAGE

In order to run a successful, scalable marketing operation, you'll need to hire experts from the outside *and* designate managers from within to be in charge of different areas of your efforts. I recommend that you have an onsite social media manager, someone who's employed by the dealership, who manages the official brand accounts and is keenly aware that social media is comprised of five major elements: listening, content strategy, community engagement, promotion, and analytics. These elements are inter-related, and a social media manager is responsible for understanding and managing them.

I don't recommend that dealerships run multiple social media accounts on the same platform. In other words, don't have one Facebook page for your dealership as a whole, one for your hybrid vehicles, one for your trucks, and one for pre-owned inventory. Many times, dealerships mistakenly think that this approach might be more effective because they believe that each account is segmenting a specific demographic with specific needs. The fact is, this approach creates massive confusion for everyone. It's incredibly complicated to manage and creates fragmentation in your brand. Your brand offers all of these products, and part of your content strategy has to involve posting about and creating interest in your brand as a whole, which includes all of the products and services that you offer.

You can maximize vehicle-specific posts by re-targeting visitors to specific pages of your website. In short, create a single profile on each strategically chosen platform as the face of your business. This will allow you to manage your social media presence in the most efficient manner. You can absolutely create social accounts on a variety of different platforms, but be wary of creating more accounts than your team can effectively manage at any point in time.

When I began working on the marketing efforts at Charles Maund, I was one of only two people at the dealership who interacted with the agencies we were partnered with. We had an internal marketing department made up of one employee, Dale Duke, and he and I worked together from the beginning of my involvement. I've learned a lot about the fundamentals of marketing from Dale. I learned from him—and he from me—and we quickly began to figure out what was working, what wasn't working, and what to do moving forward.

We had an external agency that was responsible for our TV and radio ads, and as "luck" would have it, our owner's daughter had gone to school with Andrew Street, who was one of the founders of Dealer OMG (then called Four Kicks Media). Andrew had worked directly for Facebook for about four months. He ultimately left to start his own agency, and we were their first car dealership client. The owner's daughter now works full-time for Dealer OMG and is in charge of Charles Maund's Google Ads and YouTube Ads in addition to their Facebook ads.

When I started, we also had an agency that was responsible for our TV and radio ads, but no one was focused on any other area of our marketing strategy. I alone ran point on voice mail, SMS, and phone calls, which was absolutely a full-time job in and of itself. In an ideal world, a dealership would have one person in charge of each marketing area or a combination of areas that closely relate (such as Facebook and Instagram). Since many dealerships start out needing to be a bit crafty, the best approach is to identify which platforms and approaches will provide the most bang for your buck and start with those as your skeleton effort. It's better to put more energy into a few cost-effective areas such as social media ads than spread your energy out over more expensive and time-consuming ones such as TV, radio, and billboards.

KNOW WHO'S IN CHARGE

**It's estimated that approximately 89% of messages sent by customers to brands via social media go unnoticed**

THE UNFAIR ADVANTAGE

Long term, I highly recommend hiring a marketing manager and/or designating a dedicated social media team within your marketing department. Social media managers are responsible for communicating and interacting with customers through the social media account (or accounts) for which they are responsible. It's estimated that approximately 89% of messages sent by customers to brands via social media (either through a messenger service or posted directly to your feed) go unnoticed, so it's critical that someone is responsible for checking for and responding to such messages. By being (or becoming) aware of the most common issues customers face as well as the most productive ways to resolve them, social media managers will quickly become an integral part of positively branding your dealership and encouraging new as well as repeat visitors. Any time a satisfied customer leaves positive feedback on your Facebook wall or tags you in a social media post, it's extremely helpful for the social media manager to publicly appreciate that feedback!

Another position I highly recommend is an in-house graphic designer to ensure that your graphics are branded consistently. It's rare to see a dealership with an in-house graphic designer, but it's as easy to create brand inconsistency and confusion as it is to create consistency. Many times, if your graphic designer is yet another outsourced individual or agency, you've simply created an additional layer of people who need to be able to be consistent with brand messaging through graphics (not to mention available when you need them to create a new graphic for an ad-hoc campaign you'd like to launch quickly).

Many dealerships don't, at the time they start creating a solid marketing strategy, have an employee they can allocate full-time to their marketing efforts or the budget to hire one immediately. When this is the case, I advise that dealerships allocate someone part-time to the one or two areas that are generating cost-effective results. In an attempt to save money, some businesses avoid hiring a social media team for as long as they can. As a consequence, they are unable to meet their social media goals. Experienced social media managers have a strong grip on social accounts management and can communicate with customers in an efficient way. They can present creative ideas to improve your social media strategy and respond to messages from customers in a timely manner. If you're low on budget, you can opt for a single social media manager who can manage different social accounts for the dealership. However, don't overburden your employees if you don't wish to compromise their overall productivity and performance.

It's important not to look at putting someone (or a team) in this role as a cost to your business. It's an investment. With a successful marketing strategy, your dealership can actually enhance the productivity of employees. When a marketing strategy is being executed effectively, customers come into the dealership already aware of the products and services you offer.

Sales staff, therefore, doesn't have to invest as much time convincing those customers to make a purchase. Hiring a solid in-house marketing team can also help resolve one of the major problems of society: unemployment. Marketing opens opportunities for talented social media managers, photographers, and graphic designers.

Many dealerships strive to find one agency that can handle everything (including graphic design). This makes sense in theory, but in reality most agencies that "do it all" lack strong skills in each area. When an agency tells me that they "do it all," my first question is, "How big is your agency?" It needs to be quite robust in order for me to trust that they can handle every area of a dealership's marketing strategy with the same level of knowledge and professionalism.

## RECOMMENDED AGENCY REQUIREMENTS

When we set out to hire an agency at Charles Maund, there were four requirements that had to be met just to get in the door to be able to work with us.

First, the agency had to know someone I'd worked with, preferably a top dealer I respect. This whole industry is based on relationships. If an agency owner has built a solid relationship with someone in the industry whom I respect, it gives me confidence that they understand the unique marketing needs of car dealerships.

Second, I required a monthly audit with any agency we're working with. It had to be a face-to-face call or meeting. Email wasn't sufficient. I needed to see what our performance was doing month-to-month and be able to ask questions about it.

Third, the agency had to be agile. If Snapchat use tanked when our entire strategy for attracting University of Texas students was based on Snapchat, I needed someone who could immediately say, "That's okay, we're filtering from Snapchat to something else." No agency has to manage all of the platforms

—in fact I prefer that they don't—but the platforms they do manage cannot be on autopilot. There's no "Let's setup the campaign and then head to Bali while it's running perfectly on its own" option. The digital world is constantly evolving. If your marketing strategy and team aren't agile, you'll have a hard time making the necessary modifications to update marketing images, copy, and calls to action. Furthermore, an agile approach increases the overall productivity of the marketing team. Statistics suggest that marketers can accomplish up to a 40% increase in productivity simply by being willing to take an agile approach to their social media campaigns.

Fourth, the agency must know the city- and state-specific rules regarding marketing and advertising. Insurance agencies, as an example, can lose their licenses for not following these rules. I can't tell you how many times we've been told, "This approach works so well. Let us show you how effective it is; it's absolutely legal," and then the DMV contacts us and let's us know we've done something that's *not* legal. Every city's and state's rules are different. You can't just go to a website and get correct information. There are rules and regulations for voicemails, SMS, and direct mail that have to be complied with. As a dealership, in order to contact customers via SMS, we have to have done business with them. Meaning, they have to have made a purchase or come to us for service. They can't have simply come into to take a test drive or called or emailed us with a question about whether or not we have a vehicle in stock.

# STRATEGY WINS—EVEN WHEN IT LOSES

A t the foundational level, every facet of a dealership has to be working in tandem in order for the dealership to reach its ultimate potential for success. The marketing has to be on point. The salespeople have to be on point. The owner has to let people experiment and do their thing.

## OVERALL MARKETING STRATEGY

Once you've begun humanizing your dealership, working on getting the word out about your dealership brand, and have a team (internal and/or external) in charge of your marketing strategy, it's time to get down to creating and executing on a solid overall marketing strategy. Nowadays, a majority of businesses use social media platforms for advertising due to the plethora of benefits it offers as well as its lower cost. However, not many business people are aware of the importance of having a clear social media strategy as part of your overall marketing playbook. Doing so ensures you save advertising expenses and provide a more personal and memorable experience to your customers.

Although traditional methods of advertising help businesses attract customers and increase sales, they are quite expensive. As a consequence, small businesses suffer since they cannot afford to promote their brand through these marketing tactics. Social media allows small businesses to make their place in today's competitive market and increase revenue. Large businesses can also use these platforms to further grow their business without spending a huge sum of money.

When I work with other dealerships to improve the success of their marketing efforts, the first thing I do is ask to see their written strategy. I can tell a lot about what's standing in the way of a dealership's success right there. Charles Maund's marketing playbook is broken down by platform: radio, TV, OTT, all web lead providers, direct mail, SMS, social media marketing, etc. I knew exactly how much money was being invested into each area. When I can look at another dealership's marketing playbook, I can see what platforms they do and don't have in play as well as where they're spending the majority of their budget. We can then fairly quickly reallocate their budget to be more effective. I've developed a health plan by which I can shore up business and increase sales from Day 1 when working with another dealership. More than anything else, it's simply knowing what to do and doing it without overthinking it.

I borderline insist that a dealership has one person in-house who's responsible for marketing or being the liaison to the outside marketing agency or agencies. I personally looked at our traffic every single day to see if it was up or down from a year-by-year perspective. I recently asked someone I greatly admire about his traffic report for this year versus last year and how he was measuring that to move the needle. He didn't know what I was referring to. By using this day-to-day view compared to the previous year's approach, I was able to say to Charles Maund's owner a couple of years ago, "We could simply spend the same amount of money this year, but focus on improving our process and increasing our close ratio in order to sell more cars and make more money." That's what we focused on. And we sold more cars and made more money than we had the year before, by far.

Another thing I do is check out what kind of traffic dealerships have coming to their website and how well that traffic is converting to leads. Most dealerships are aware of that information, but many don't have it organized. It's important for me to see what their year-to-year comparison is because if they're selling more cars than the previous year, it may be because their traffic is up—or it may be that they're doing a better job marketing. If a dealership has sold more cars this year than last year and it's because they're doing a better job at selling, that's one thing. If they're selling more because their traffic is higher, that's another. There may be ways to improve their sales process to increase the close ratio. This also helps a dealership assess whether they have too many or not enough sales people on the floor.

When I first got to Charles Maund, there were two guys in the Internet department, and the rest were on the sales floor. That was the way it had always been. It wasn't until later on that we started to recognize that we needed more people on the floor to manage incoming traffic from ads. It's important to constantly be monitoring that. My rule of thumb is, if I'm funneling all my internet traffic to the BDC, there is generally a 2:1 ratio of leads to phone calls. So if I've got two leads, I'll have at least one incoming phone call. I need to make sure my sales guys are only getting 40-50 leads or else they'll have too many customers to effectively manage.

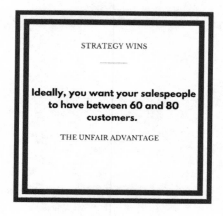

STRATEGY WINS

**Ideally, you want your salespeople to have between 60 and 80 customers.**

THE UNFAIR ADVANTAGE

Ideally, you want your salespeople to have between 60 and 80 total customers (including both ongoing customers and walk-in customers). You can then work to do a better job on communicating with (retaining) and closing those customers. An average of 10% of leads will close, so with 60-80 customers, we could reliably project that we'd sell 6-8 cars. If we weren't doing that, we worked with our customer base a little bit more up-front and were then mindful of our follow-up. When we maximized our efforts with targeted traffic, we were generally able to close 15-20 sales for every 60-80 leads.

Sometimes, dealerships put the cart before the horse. They believe their issue is that they need to sell more vehicles when, in fact, the issue is that they have more leads than they have salespeople to effectively handle those leads (or their salespeople aren't properly managing the leads they're getting). There has to be a match between the appropriate number of salespeople, marketing people, and outside agencies to correlate with the amount of traffic that a dealership is driving from ads. It times time, attention, and finesse to get these ratios to the most effective level.

Another variable is whether or not the dealership has only one location or multiple locations. When they're trying to spread their overall reach across a number of locations, their reach and frequency may not be as effective as those that have only one location. If a dealership is divvying out a $300,000 marketing budget between ten locations versus allotting it all to one location, there's going to be a measurable difference in reach and frequency. When you have multiple locations, you want to have effective branding as a group, but you need to be strategic in your marketing and the ways in which you're retaining your customers at each location. I believe it's important to look at ways to retain current customers *first*, before deploying money toward the acquisition of new customers. Branding to and acquisition of new customers is more expensive than continuing to serve and market to current customers in almost any business. Once you get a handle on your processes, it's easy to add a little bit here and a little bit there to create a natural marketing progression.

It's important to honestly assess how controlling the dealership owner is over marketing. If an owner is doing so well financially that he chooses to hire out the full array of marketing efforts, it's critical that he hires the best agency or agencies for the job. If not, it's critical that he's involved and/or has the right people at the dealership involved. Otherwise, the store's growth will begin to trend backward, which is an expensive mistake. Pay the right people from the beginning. You'll get what you pay for.

STRATEGY WINS

**Pay the right people from the beginning. You'll get what you pay for.**

THE UNFAIR ADVANTAGE

The biggest mistake I see is that dealerships simply aren't paying attention. When I worked at CarMax years ago, we had a term for employees who had become extremely complacent. We called them "5 Year Managers." Once they'd been in their role for five years or so, they simply became complacent. They got comfortable with the plateau they'd reached and weren't motivated to take things to the next level. One of the smartest things a dealership can do once they've hit a plateau as a whole is bring in an outside expert to see what's missing. Even we did that! We got stuck on a plateau a couple of years ago. I brought someone in to assess the situation as an outsider and see where the gaps were. We were able to turn things around quickly, and I'll never again make the mistake of thinking I can figure it out on my own if only I think harder. At some point, the fastest route to the next level is someone with fresh eyes.

## REASONS DEALERSHIPS DON'T IMPLEMENT

Dealerships often worry about dependencies. For example, they worry, *Will these strategies only work if we have a $100,000 per month marketing budget? Or 50,000 customers in our database? Or a Facebook following of at least 5,000?* The strategies I employ tend to work no matter what because they focus on establishing a unique, solid foundation upon which a successful strategy can be built and scaled. Saying, "We don't have enough money for a true strategy" is simply a copout. If a dealership has a limited budget, my advice is to, first and foremost, make sure they have lead providers such as cargurus.com and cars.com. Those providers are already spending money to be in front of customers. I'd then get rid of TV and other super expensive platforms. I'd suggest focusing on a digital strategy first and proceeding from there.

One challenge I see again and again is that dealerships are making things too hard for themselves. The first thing I frequently do when working to help another dealership increase their numbers is simply look at the number of leads coming in and ensure that the dealership has enough people managing those leads. There's no big secret strategy here; dealerships simply have too many leads coming in for the number of salespeople they have managing them. Owners say to me, "I have a huge number of leads," but when we start looking at the lead management and paying attention, what's really going on behind the scenes becomes clearer. It doesn't make sense, for example, to have one salesperson take care of 100 customers when they can be most effective taking care of 40 or 50. Dealerships often look for a magic bullet, but the truth is that it's about putting in the work and being really clear on what's going on and why, not simply what could be going better.

If you're starting small, that's okay. I say it's like eating an elephant; you do it one bite at a time. That's how you avoid becoming overwhelmed. We first look at what a dealership is doing *right*. It's not always about tossing everything out and starting over from scratch. We identify what's working and keep doing that, and we identify what's *not* working and replace it. Many times, the first step is tweaking something that's already working well just a tiny bit in order to take your results to the next level.

We take the time to determine where a dealership's traffic is coming from. Once you know where your traffic is coming from, you can determine how that compares year-over-year and make some intelligent decisions on where to put your marketing dollars and/or focus on sales training.

We used Spyfu to explore traffic on competitors' websites. Spyfu and similar services have both free and paid versions that allow you to visit your competitor's website in order to see where their referral traffic is coming from. You can see their digital game plan, to a degree. We'll see where their top referrals are coming from as well as what keywords are bringing traffic to a competitor's website. Depending on the cost of those keywords through Google AdsWords, we may begin using them as well to get in front of some of the competition's traffic.

## BE AWARE

Downtime is going to occur. Don't simply bow to downtime and use it as an excuse to sit back and watch cartoons in the dealership while you're waiting for a situation to resolve itself. For example, In 2008 I was working at Universal Toyota. I'd left CarMax to work at Universal on the sales floor because I heard about how much money was available to be made in sales. The first financial crisis to hit *us* specifically was the "sticky pedal" incident. Someone was on the news saying that their pedal had gotten stuck in the accelerate position. I believe they ultimately came to find out that it was a floor mat issue—the floor mat got stuck holding the pedal down. During the investigation, however, we were not allowed to sell any Toyota vehicles. I knew I had to sell cars as a salesperson, so I had to figure it out.

Because we couldn't sell any cars, I had to focus on what I *could* sell because my family still needed to eat! I manually scrubbed our lists of customers who'd purchased a vehicle from us. I still managed to sell 30 cars that month while everyone else sat around waiting for us to have permission to start selling again. We couldn't sell new cars, but we could sell pre-owned vehicles, so that's what I focused on. There were also certain vehicles that came directly from Japan that we could sell. Some 4Runners and Corollas were included in this; as long as they came from Japan they could be sold because those factories used a different pedal. I lined up all the cars we could sell and told my manager to put them as close to the front of the lot as possible. I didn't think I'd be able to sell all of them—there were 15 black Corollas lined up side-by-side—but I sold 10 or 11 of them. While everyone else was singing the blues, I went to work.

Gary Vee often talks about the importance of awareness, and I think some people simply don't use their awareness to their advantage. I can see when something's about to go down, and I find that most people can do that very well if they are paying attention. For example, I can look at my one-year-old and think, "Man, this guy's gonna fall," or "He's about to eat something he shouldn't eat." It's about not being somewhere without actually *being* there, which we all do from time to time. It's about honing the skill of being aware of what's happening around you and how you can impactfully respond.

## AUTOPILOT DOESN'T WORK

Quite simply, your marketing efforts can never be put on autopilot. Even if you have the help of a software program like The AutoMiner, the human component of making sure that the right strategies are being executed can never be fully removed. Everyone involved has to be agile. The world changes every single day. Look at Vine, for example. Or Snapchat. Snapchat made one update and the whole platform tanked (for a moment). But for those whose marketing campaigns were dependent upon Snapchat, without a marketing team that was agile enough to pivot quickly, a great deal of money was lost.

STRATEGY WINS

**Quite simply, your marketing efforts can never be put on autopilot.**

THE UNFAIR ADVANTAGE

## SOCIAL MEDIA STRATEGY

It's a prevalent misconception among dealerships that their customer base can be increased simply by establishing an online presence and inundating followers with content. This is far from factual. Of course it's essential for every business, especially car dealerships, to maintain an online presence. A professional website is a must, however a website alone isn't enough to significantly increase sales. Dealerships must find ways to increase the traffic to their website and then convert that traffic into customers.

Approximately 2.5 billion people actively use social media worldwide. It's not easy (it may not even be possible) and it's certainly not profitable to target that entire user base with a single marketing campaign. Segmentation allows you to target smaller groups of people to increase sales to your ideal customers. You can segment your audience on the basis of their priorities, interests, income level, education level, and many other parameters. Social media uses behavioral targeting and retargeting to track down the interests and needs of your target market, and a bit of time spent researching the preferences of your most frequent customers will help you more fully understand exactly what he or she is all about.

Before the internet came into existence, it was difficult for dealerships to get in touch with customers. They relied heavily on surveys to solicit feedback but were only able to contact and interact with a small portion of their customers with this approach. Social media marketing provides them with the opportunity to easily stay in touch with a wide range of customers via a wide variety of platforms. While dealerships continue to promote their brand, products, and services via a variety of online and digital methods such as voicemail advertising, online advertising, print advertising, broadcast advertising, and Over The Top media, although these methods are effective, they cannot compete with the benefits of social media when it comes to attracting customers.

Approximately 88% of businesses in the U.S. have a presence on social media sites such as Facebook, Instagram, LinkedIn, and YouTube. However, not every business understands the importance of having a clearly defined social media marketing strategy as part of their overall marketing strategy. They either omit the step of developing a strategy altogether or create an ineffective one that fails them. I can't tell you the number of times I've heard, "Social media marketing just doesn't work for us." It's not that it doesn't work, it's that it doesn't work the way it's been set up. With a proper strategy, execution and patience, I've yet to encounter a dealership that can't benefit tremendously from social media advertising. When it was first suggested that we use Facebook to advertise Charles Maund, I was perhaps the most skeptical of all. I couldn't believe that there was any way we could sell cars off of Facebook. I was proven wrong over and over again.

During the early years of social media, many businesses considered it a waste of time to use these platforms for business promotions. This is no longer the case. Today, social media serves as one of the most inexpensive ways to effectively reach customers. If you search online for car dealerships, you'll likely discover that many of your competitors are already using Facebook, Instagram, Twitter, and other online platforms to attract and retain customers. Dealerships that are active *and* have a defined strategy on prominent social platforms have the greatest success grabbing customers' attention.

Even though most businesses now understand the importance of these platforms and use them to reach out to customers, it's not as common as you might think for them to have a documented social media strategy. A social media strategy is a series of actions or steps through which you plan to meet the goals you've set in your overall marketing plan. The strategy defines actions you need to perform in order to increase sales, attract more customers, retain those customers, and keep them engaged with useful and entertaining content. Having a documented strategy assists in-house marketers as well as outside agencies in planning, prioritizing, executing, measuring, and optimizing any and all social media campaigns.

Without formally documenting your goals and objectives, it won't be easy to meet them. As Peter Drucker said, "If you can't measure it, you can't improve it." Whether you run a small car dealership or own a large automotive company, don't delay the creation of an intentional social media strategy to promote your brand in the most effective manner.

A social media strategy can be developed in many ways. First, determine which social media channels your customers frequent, and incorporate them into your strategy. Compared to more traditional forms of advertising and alternative digital marketing channels such as direct mail, TV, radio, banner ads, Google AdWords, and billboard campaigns, social media marketing campaigns are far more cost-effective. In such a competitive market, you don't want to lose the race, and if your competitors have a solid social media strategy in place, it won't take them long to attract your customer base via their social media platforms.

An effective marketing strategy is created with the help of thorough market research. Such research gives insight into, for example, popular hashtags related to your industry. It also aids employees in understanding how best to communicate with current as well as prospective customers and what types of content are most effective on different social media platforms. Social media is vital when it comes to customer retention, as it enables companies to keep their customers engaged and make them feel valued. That kind of customer engagement builds strong rapport and earns customer loyalty.

That said, it isn't easy to most effectively communicate with your customers without researching the types of content that resonate with them. Conducting such research can shed light on popular topics to speak to or provide information about. Furthermore, it helps you to understand ways you can promote your business subtly so that customers don't become annoyed by repetitive advertisements.

Part of your overall strategy must be a willingness to come up with content on-the-fly. Always be on the lookout for opportunities to communicate and engage. Everyone at Charles Maund is encouraged to make suggestions at any time if they have sudden inspiration when it comes to a Facebook Live, video, or text post.

As far as a budget for these one-the-fly campaigns, plan for it up front. I ensured that we had an extra $5,000 budgeted specifically for on-the-fly ads. Every dealership should have this category as part of their social media marketing budget. Glen Lundy, who is GM of a dealership in Paris, Kentucky, is always looking at what's happening on social media and will then do his own version of it. Because he has no idea when or how often these sorts of opportunities will present themselves, they become part of the on-the-fly budget. An example of this is Will Smith, who took on the #InMyFeelingsChallenge by dancing to a Drake song on a bridge with a drone flying overhead filming it. Glen thought it was a fun approach and did his version of it at his dealership, racking up over 11,000 organic views. Sometimes you don't even have to invest to push it. You get what I call "organic virality."

*Sidenote: Be sure that your the reason you're inspired by someone else's approach is in line with your brand and overall goals. Replicating something simply because it's trendy or went viral rarely works and, in some cases, can have a detrimental effect.*

Speaking of trends, many dealerships make the mistake of creating social media campaigns based simply on trends. That's their actual strategy. It's easy to hear, "You've got to start using chatbots" or "Periscope is amazing for business." However, the success of your marketing campaign lies in a long-term plan combined with a solid understanding of your dealership—what its brand is about, where it is, and where it's going—as well as your ideal customers. If you don't have that knowledge *combined with* a solid strategy, your efforts to engage with customers may, in fact, backfire and cost you quite a bit of time and money in the process. Beware of jumping on a new trend without doing your due diligence. It's critical to ensure that the approach makes sense for *your dealership* at any particular point in time.

It wasn't until I understood the Rule of 7 that I was able to create content that was successful regardless of whether or not it was trendy. If I could create content around a specific goal, only then did I see a lift in what I was trying to accomplish—regardless of how trendy the approach was or wasn't at the time. If i just posted random ads, I would get some engagement but not the kind of engagement that's possible when you have a specific goal communicated several different ways. The pitch is exactly the same; it's just presented in seven different ways.

## CRITICAL TOUCHPOINTS

A brand's touchpoints represent any manner through which customers come into contact with the brand. When dealerships develop their social media strategy, they must consider those touchpoints in order to reap maximum benefits. Your social media strategy should focus on the first impression you make on a potential customer. There's no way you'll get a second chance to improve a bad first impression. Build a social media profile that is likely to grab the attention of your ideal customers as soon as they visit it.

Keep in mind the following customer path: Know, Like, Trust, Try, Buy, Repeat. The first thing a customer has to do is *know* about you. If he's impressed with your brand at first sight, chances are he'll be interested in learning more, and quite possibly, becoming a customer down the road. For this reason, it's critical to ensure that your social profile stands out from the competition.

Once a user knows of you, they have to decide that they *like* you. When developing a social media strategy for your dealership, make sure you take into account the values and preferences of your customers. Customers will quickly become annoyed if you flood them with nothing but advertisements. Social media users like interesting stories. So develop interesting content such as videos, infographics, polls, and other interactive content to build their interest and engage them.

Once they know and like you, users have to *trust* you. The key to building strong ties with your customer base is to increase their trust in you over time. Social media users are prone to reading customer reviews of a brand or service. Encourage your satisfied customers to leave positive feedback on your social media pages. The more positive reviews you receive, the more leads they'll generate.

Once you have know, like, and trust down, it's time to *try* to attract potential customers with targeted offers and deals or a free test drive.

An effective social media strategy will then take the user to the *buy* phase. When customers are in the process of making a buying decision, they want to see content that assures them they're making the right choice. This is a great reason to post content that includes the experiences of satisfied customers.

Video testimonials work incredibly well if you have a customer who is willing to provide one. Think about accident attorneys for a moment. They use video testimonials all the time. The video notes that the person in it is an actual client, and the client is prompted to speak to all of the aspects of hiring an accident attorney that most people have objections to or fears over. They speak to the way they were treated like a human being, the great communication the law firm had with them, and the fact that they felt truly taken care of. When the prospect sees him or herself in the customer or the customer's experience, the impact is even higher.

Your work isn't finished once a customer has purchased a vehicle. Not even close. You must retain them in order to make your business successful. Therefore, a portion of your social media strategy *must* focus on customer service. The better the customer service, the stronger your relationship with customers. 71% of customers break ties with a brand simply because of unsatisfactory customer service. Beyond potential customers, your social media strategy must focus on your long-term, loyal consumers. With efficient customer support, you'll keep them around for a long time. You can also convert them into advocates for your business. If they're satisfied with your services, they'll likely spread word of your dealership and defend your brand on social media.

Every marketing plan requires some level of financial investment. While documenting your goals, make sure you have your quarterly or annual budget in mind. If necessary, you can even pitch your overall marketing strategy and needs to investors in order to obtain additional funding.

Experts suggest using a SMART framework when coming up with effective goals. SMART stands for:

- Specific
- Measurable
- Attainable

- Relevant
- Timely

A single social media strategy can and will be comprised of various goals. However, make sure that your goals meet the above specified criteria. The major purpose of creating a marketing strategy is to reach out to customers. While the main goal of a social media strategy is reaching your target audience, you can't effectively accomplish that goal unless you know a good bit about your target audience. Your social media strategy should clarify your target customer in solid detail.

It's important to be more specific than you likely imagine up front when brainstorming about the details of your target audience. You may want to target them on the basis of location, income, job title, age, most-used social networks, or challenges they're experiencing in their life. And you must be able to speak directly to them in your ads. For instance, one ad campaign may have a goal of selling luxury cars to executives with a high income and another may have a goal of selling hybrid vehicles in a specific environmentally conscious city.

No matter how creative your marketing content is, you won't get your desired results and meet your marketing goals if you don't have clarity on who each ad is intended to speak to. Clarifying your target audience will help you satisfy their needs and effectively introduce offers of interest to them. It allows you to effectively provide solutions to your ideal customers' main challenges. For instance, if your target audience is challenged by a financial inability to purchase an expensive car, you can target them with an ad for a small, hybrid car that not only saves them money on gasoline costs but makes their commute easier by allowing them to travel in the HOV lane and possibly qualifies them for a tax deduction.

## SOCIAL MEDIA AUDIT

If you already have a professional social account or accounts for your dealership, you need to conduct a social media audit before launching into the creation of a social media strategy. Conducting an audit allows you to assess the impact your brand is having on a the different platforms it's active on. Take the time to evaluate how you currently communicate with your customers, and consider customer feedback that's already present on your social media pages.

I always looked at my competitors in terms of what they are doing in the space. I looked at what approaches they were trying that might have worked for us, looked to see how many views they were getting, etc. It takes work. There's unfortunately no real quick snapshot or health report you can get in order to see immediately who your competitors are, what they're doing, and how well it's working.

Dealerships tend to focus too heavily at first on the number of followers they have and the number of Likes their posts are receiving. Further, dealerships with a large following often mistakenly believe that a high number of followers sets them up for a successful social media campaign—even if those followers aren't engaged. That belief is highly inaccurate. If users ignore your posts, it's not a good sign. It communicates that your posts are boring or your customers cannot view the posts on their timeline. The Facebook algorithm naturally shows users more of what they like, so if they don't often like your posts, Facebook won't even show them to them organically any longer. Therefore, you need to come up with an effective strategy to increase visibility, engage customers with valuable content, and retain them for the long term.

Choose platforms you're committed to continuing with and keep your eye out for pages that may be copying your brand name or content. Fake social pages will occasionally pop up to defame your business. Should this happen, report them as soon as possible.

It's critical to build your social media strategy around your brand's values. Create a list of your brand's core values and mission statement and develop your social media strategy accordingly. Your social media strategy should focus on ways to benefit current and prospective customers within a specified time frame. As a dealership, it's critical to ensure that you're promoting your message the proper way. For instance, if you deal in hybrid cars only, spread awareness about the environmental and other benefits of hybrid vehicles. Deliver the message that you sell these cars because they provide more better mileage and are eco-friendly.

On the flip side, if you sell hybrid cars simply because they are in demand, your social media plan may not yield your desired sales results. You're not the only car dealership out there. In the vicinity of your dealership, there are likely a number of additional dealerships. Further, if your goal is to target a national or a global audience, competition will be high. In order to stand out from the crowd, you'll have to provide something to your followers that your competition isn't offering. If your marketing strategy is similar to that of your competitors, it's not wise to expect to catch much attention. Come up with a unique and more valuable approach that is likely to become the center of your followers' attention in this space.

It can be tempting to attempt to copy a successful competitor's social media strategy, but don't. It never works. Just like in high school, you can copy what someone else does, but if you don't understand the nuts and bolts of their foundation and why they've chosen their approach, you won't understand it well enough to scale it or use it as the foundation for another campaign (or the next math lesson)! Take the time to craft and hone a strategy that's unique to your dealership and customers. It will have a much more profitable lasting impact and be far less frustrating in the long-term.

## HAVE A CALL TO ACTION

Without a clear CTA (Call To Action), social media content quickly becomes useless. While developing your social media strategy, plan for the most suitable CTAs that will work for you. If you have trouble coming up with a useful CTA, it'll be almost impossible to engage customers and convince them to share their thoughts on your text posts or visual content.

A CTA can include a request to comment on a specific question, a link to sign up for a tip sheet, a link to a page on your website, or a link to schedule a service appointment. The possibilities are almost endless, but make sure that, when you're crafting your content, you're asking yourself, "What do I want a follower to *do* after reading this post" and make sure the CTA supports that.

## INDUSTRY EVENTS

Industry events can be invaluable, especially if you are extremely clear on your reasons for attending prior to going. Attending events simply to attend rarely nets valuable results. Most events I attend at this point aren't ones wherein dealers are looking to purchase new products, per se. Instead, they are going to learn (or re-learn) abut what's new as well as what's up-and-coming in terms of technology, sales approaches, and retention strategies in order to help their dealership both today and in the future. Being at these events gives you an opportunity to take a second look at a product you may have heard about in the past or catch up on the evolution of a product or technology you looked into the past.

These sorts of event are geared toward a combination of two intentions: showcasing new vendors and technologies available to help dealers and workshops designed to assist a dealership's internet/BDC and sales & service teams.

## 6 Benefits of Intentionally Attending Industry Events

*Meet the Decision Makers*

B2B events allow you the opportunity to meet key decision-makers face-to-face. Relationships rule the roost in this and almost every other industry, and if you can strategically plan to meet with the decision makers you're most focused on, it can go a long way toward forging a solid, long-term relationship. Many attendees will have their days mapped out well ahead of time, so if there is a decision-maker or influencer you are committed to connecting with, approach them in advance of the event via LinkedIn, email, or another platform and invite them to join you for coffee or lunch.

*MAKE NEW CONNECTIONS*

Again, it's all about relationships. Your circle will only expand into the circle of your network, so it's important to choose that network wisely. While you may attend an event with the intention of meeting a few specific people, you also simply never know who you may run into "by accident" and forget a strong and mutually beneficial connection. Make sure that you get contact information for each person you meet *when you meet them.* Thinking that you'll catch up with them later in the event to grab that information often backfires, as everyone's schedule changes by the hour, and these events come to a close far more quickly than we initially imagine.

*FORM NEW PARTNERSHIPS*

There have certainly been instances wherein people meet at events or conferences and choose to partner up in some way. Perhaps they serve a similar audience with different products and can cross-market one another through an affiliate relationship. Or, someone has an area of expertise that you are in need of and vice versa and you can connect for knowledge exchange and support down the line.

### SEE WHAT'S ON THE HORIZON

Big events and conferences typically feature up-and-coming technology and products, and it can be extremely beneficial to be on the leading edge of knowledge when it comes to new opportunities, even if you don't buy in to them right away. Knowing what's coming gives you the advantage of being able to incorporate that knowledge into your sales strategies and marketing plans so that you don't feel behind the 8-ball.

### PERCEPTION

You know the saying, perception is often reality. When you attend events and conferences, you appear to be in-the-know and a heavy hitter in your industry. It subconsciously communicates that you truly have a strong interest in what you do and either you or your company believes in you enough to fund your attendance of the event. Social proof from such events (photos, quotes, lessons learned) also help to increase your authority and credibility in your field. But again, don't think that simply attending an event is going to up that authority and credibility for more than a few minutes. You must truly go with the intention of connecting with new people and learning about new ways to make a bigger impact in the marketplace.

### SEE WHAT THE COMPETITION IS DOING

In the automobile industry, keep in mind that your competition isn't necessarily your day-to-day competition. For example, if you work at a Toyota dealership in Austin, Texas and you connect with someone who works at or runs a Toyota dealership in Maine, you aren't competing for the same audience even though you sell the same product. Therefore, you can forge a relationship of cooperation where you share strategies and approaches while helping each other with your respective challenges.

## OTT

While the potential for advertising on social media is massive, it's important not to invest your dealership's entire marketing budget in that area. Dealerships that rely solely on social media, overlooking other forms of marketing such as print or broadcast marketing, typically begin losing customers. In order to make your social media strategy powerful, decide on an overall marketing budget, and then commit only a portion of it to social media campaigns.

One of the latest strategies to hit the scene is OTT (Over-The-Top) advertising, which refers to platforms such as Hulu, Netflix, and other streaming services. It's a fast-growing approach across multiple industries because it brings attention to a brand in a way no other form of advertising does.

On-demand channels, streaming services, and DVR technology are here to stay, and the platforms are expected to significantly expand in the coming years. Since the future of OTT advertising is quite bright, now is the perfect time to begin building your knowledge about and investing in these channels in order to future-proof your business.

Consumers' attention has become extremely fragmented. Their attention used to be focused solely on TV and radio. Now it's spread out over cable, Hulu, social media accounts, Facebook Watch, Instagram, and YouTube (for starters). OTT puts quick commercials—sometimes only 5-10 seconds—in areas where a commercial slot is available, especially in Facebook Watch or YouTube content, and marketers have to be strategic about how to get their message out in that short a span of time.

Before adopting the OTT method, however, you must—first and foremost—understand what it actually is and how to most effectively use it. OTT advertising targets users of VOD (Video On Demand) platforms, which are flourishing. Instead of waiting for hours to watch their favorite TV shows, viewers can view anything, anytime, via on-demand channels. Once they create a simple account, they can binge watch their favorite movies or TV shows through a paid monthly subscription. Users can watch content on-the-go via their mobile device, computer, or TV. They can often even download it to watch later. This technology is also used by many airlines to entertain travelers while in flight.

More than 65% of the world's population watches VOD content. Brands can increase brand visibility and awareness simply by signing a contract to display commercials on these platforms. That said, OTT advertising isn't as simple as it initially seems. You must first get a solid grasp on the unique features of each platform in order to efficiently and cost-effectively expand your customer base through adverting on it. There is no way to programmatically access the ad inventory, so businesses need to work harder and smarter to reach their target audience.

Assuming that every single one of the VOD platforms is the right fit for any one dealership is a mistake. While these platforms are said to be the future of advertising, not many businesses are currently using these channels to promote their content—or at least they aren't using them as effectively as they could be. The earlier you learn to properly utilize the most appropriate VOD channels to promote your dealership, the faster you'll get an upper hand over your competitors and possibly even win over a portion of their established customer base.

One of the benefits of advertising via OTT is that the rates are based on CPM accounting, which allows dealerships to make decisions that enable their investment to more strongly benefit their business. Global events such as the Olympic Games and natural disasters tend to affect the behavior of viewers, compelling them to be more interested in watching sports or news channels, for example.

OTT advertising is the future of marketing for many reasons, not the least of which is that it provides opportunities for dealerships to cut down on marketing expenses by increasing brand visibility at a fraction of the cost of traditional advertising. In fact, traditional advertising costs are comparably outrageous, and businesses can easily spend all of their profit quite quickly if they aren't careful. In order to ensure that their dollars are being spent effectively, most dealers have agencies that use Spectrum or other media outlets, however they can, as a general rule, bypass those outlet and purchase directly from DataXu.

More and more people are subscribing to VOD platforms and connected to their TVs to enjoy steaming of television shows, movies, and other digital content at their own convenience. Businesses can follow this trend and promote their products and services via OTT advertising by utilizing the platforms and preferences of their ideal customers.

With so many OTT services available, it's not easy for a business to choose the right type and format for effective commercials. Users of VOD platforms can access the application via their mobile phone, gaming consoles, smart TV, or any other smart device, and every device has different resolution requirements. Some streaming devices have fixed protocols that specify that all advertisements must be in HD format, whereas other devices accept all video and audio formats. These challenges are technical in nature, and OTT service providers are working hard to develop a collective solution as quickly as possible. It's essential that network protocols and hardware requirements be standardized so that brands can promote themselves effectively. Until standard protocols are and requirements are implemented by OTT media services, mismatches will occur and businesses will incur the associated losses, which is unfortunate, but it's simply a part of the experience for now.

OTT media services also often overlook user experience. When it comes to advertising via OTT media, users are often bombarded with same ads in a single session. While some brands believe that repetition is the key to staying in a customer's mind, this practice actually often negatively impacts users and *lessens* their interest in a brand. As it's still relatively new, the OTT industry is undergoing continuous development, and during this time, effective steps must be taken by those managing OTT campaigns to streamline advertising. It's necessary to ensure that users don't become annoyed by too-often-repeated ads, which end up decreasing the value of the brand and affecting the buying decisions of customers.

## POPULAR VOD PLATFORMS

*Netflix*

One of the most popular VOD platforms is Netflix. Netflix provides access to unlimited movies, TV shows, video clips, and live videos from different parts of the world. Via its optimized interface, it easily streams through one's TV, computer, or mobile device. Compared to similar platforms, its subscription is more expensive.

*HULU*

After Netflix, the next largest host of digital content is Hulu, which comes with a lower subscription fee and access to the latest episodes of many currently on-air TV shows. However, their complete collection of TV shows and movies is relatively small compared to Netflix. Furthermore, mid-show commercials (which, for now, cannot be avoided) may annoy users.

· · ·

## AMAZON INSTANT VIDEO

Amazon Instant Video is an easy platform through which users can consume a lot of video and audio content. Its video library contains free as well as paid content. Users can add their favorite content to their library and enjoy it anytime. A subscription to Amazon Prime avails users to various additional benefits including Amazon Prime Instant Video, Amazon Music, and Kindle.

## YOUTUBE

YouTube is one of the most popular video-sharing websites, and it also maintains a comprehensive database of TV shows and movie clips obtainable through legal means. Users can watch free content in HD or SD resolutions and can also sync their account to their mobile devices in order to enjoy their favorite content anytime, anywhere.

## SLING TV

Sling TV is an online streaming platform that allows users to watch a limited number of older TV shows. It often serves as an effective replacement for cable TV. Sports enthusiasts find it attractive since it allows them to watch a variety of sports channels in real-time. For the user, however, the live sports channel streaming component comes with high subscription prices.

## CRACKLE

Crackle VOD service is backed by Sony and allows users to enjoy unlimited TV shows, movies, anime, and original "older" programming. It's a free service, but the tradeoff is that users have to suffer through long commercials (which they often will use as an opportunity to run to the kitchen for a snack because they know they have a bit of time before their content resumes).

## HBO

HBO offers two different subscriptions for its viewers: HBO GO and HBO NOW. Viewers who wish to watch on-demand programs via cable TV or satellite packages can subscribe to HBO GO. On the other hand, those more interested in premium content can become members of HBO NOW, which is a more expensive service.

## TWITCH

Passionate gamers often search for online videos showcasing their favorite games. These videos guide viewers on how to improve their skills, clear certain levels, and incorporate tips and cheats. Twitch is one of the largest such services for gamers. The platform also broadcasts talk shows where top gamers share their insights and experiences.

## VEVO

Vevo is one of the top music streaming services. In addition to streaming online music shows, it allows users to search for their favorite music videos. In fact, it's presently the only dedicated music video service that allows music fans to listen to their favorite bands. Users can watch music videos, concerts, and documentaries on the lives of people who have made it big in the music industry.

## PLAYSTATION VUE

PlayStation Vue is a top choice of viewers who want to watch live TV shows as well as record them to watch later. It's a great replacement for cable TV. This service, which is offered by Sony, gives users the freedom to choose from four subscription plans: Access, Core, Elite, and Ultra.

## COMCAST XFINITY

When it comes to VOD platforms, it's not possible to overlook the popularity of Comcast Xfinity. A subsidiary of Comcast Corporation, it's one of the highest grossing cable companies in the world. With a large collection of digital content, it allows users to choose from more than 55,000 movies or TV shows.

## GOOGLE PLAY

Google Play provides access to modern-day TV shows and movies as well as a sizable database of past content. Android users can now enjoy their favorite media content on their smart devices by either purchasing content they want to watch or renting it for a fraction of its original cost. It acquires the same wireless transmission services as Netflix to provide Android users with a smooth streaming experience.

## ITUNES

The iTunes VOD model is similar to that of Google Play. However, this service can only be accessed via Apple devices. Those who own an iPhone, iPad, MacBook, or Apple TV can purchase video or audio content and download it to watch it later at their convenience. Furthermore, the AirPlay app allows iOS users to stream content across a Wi-Fi network.

## VUDU

Vudu is a subsidiary of Walmart Stores, Inc. It's an online

content delivery service that legally transmits full-length movies via the internet. The Vudu model is quite similar to that of both Google Play and iTunes. What makes it stand out, however, is its integration with the Ultraviolet library. Users can watch any movie that they have purchased from Ultraviolet through Vudu, and they can share their digital library with up to five additional users. Another prominent feature of this service is that it is free.

## DVR

A DVR (Digital Video Recorder) is an electronic device that allows users to record digital content while it's streaming. It records content to a mass storage device so that users can watch it whenever they choose. It saves time for viewers and ensures they don't miss their favorite TV shows due to their busy schedules. DVR technology is an alternative to VOD services. The initial digital video recorder was introduced in 1999. Since then, the technology has undergone several reiterations in order to have arrived where it stands today. Nowadays, many televisions come with a built-in DVR device.

As you can see, there are a wide variety of OTT services available and certainly more on the horizon. OTT technology provides more flexibility for users, and businesses can capitalize on this technology by promoting their brand through OTT platforms.

Every dealership—whether large or small—needs to target a specific customer base in order to increase sales. Let's talk about the automotive industry specifically, since that's your area of focus. In the same way other forms of advertising can, OTT ads can be positioned to target a specific demographic or an audience with a specific lifestyle that makes them more likely engage in and complete a vehicle purchase from your dealership. Dealerships can collect this important demographic information via ratings and projections of VOD platforms. DataXu is a platform dealerships can use to target specific clients and audiences based on the demographic data of a specific platform's users. The demographic data imports a lot like that of Facebook and Instagram, but for TV.

Typically, OTT advertisements can be of varying length. However, the standard length of these ads is 15, 30, or 60 seconds. A great way to reach customers is by focusing on their immediate needs and the platforms your research shows that they are using. For instance, companies selling video games target gaming channels. Don't assume that you know where your customers are. I've seen this mistake time and time again. It's truly in your best interests (and the best interests of your overall marketing budget) to confirm or deny your assumptions through solid research so you are sure you're being as effective as possible.

When businesses pay for ad placement on a TV channel, not all their ads are viewed. Viewers tend to skip ads by switching to another channel (or grabbing that bowl of ice cream while during a commercial break). Also, when it comes to TV commercials, businesses have to rely on employees to create, schedule and manage an advertising campaign. However, when it comes to OTT advertising, businesses don't pay for advertisements that are skipped by viewers; they only pay for actual viewership of their ads.

Since several OTT platforms force viewers to watch commercials *before* they can access their desired content, businesses can be far more confident that their investment isn't going to waste. They can also be confident that the commercials are watched by a specifically targeted person. OTT platforms are usually accessed by a single person at a time via a smart device. So, instead of targeting an entire family, businesses can make their campaigns more fruitful by observing the behavior of individual users. By showing ads on different VOD platforms, advertisers can reach a wider range of potential customers in different parts of the world. The higher a brand's visibility, the easier it is for dealerships to expand their customer base.

Unlike TV and radio advertising, OTT advertising allows dealerships to monitor viewership in real-time and retrieve information about the location of viewers, the devices they are using, and much more. These statistics are extremely valuable in determining whether or not ads have reached their target audience. Additionally, while TV channels are usually watched by an entire family or multiple people at a time, OTT ads make it easier for an ads manager to know the precise number of viewers an ad is receiving and use this information to optimize and enhance their campaign strategy by logging in and monitoring the impacts of their campaign in real time.

OTT advertising campaigns also allow advertisers to launch their campaigns almost immediately. It doesn't take more than 72 hours to setup and launch a campaign to attract customers. You can upload new commercials and modify or stop a campaign that isn't generating desired results at any time.

No matter how many benefits it provides to a business, OTT advertising does pose certain challenges. Despite their increasing popularity, VOD platforms still have a long way to go. The majority of people still prefer watching movies and shows via traditional cable networks, mainly because they are unaware of the plethora of benefits that OTT media services provide. As a result, if businesses want to attract more customers and increase brand visibility via OTT, it's in their best interests to spread awareness of and promote OTT media services themselves. The more customers know about new OTT services (especially the ones a dealership is choosing to advertise with) and their advantages over traditional cable networks, the more interested they'll be in downloading and/or subscribing to the application. Not only will those subscriptions help them cut down on cable TV expenses in the long run, they'll also allow dealerships to reach a larger customer base.

## VIRTUAL REALITY

Virtual Reality is a relatively new technology. It creates an alternate environment that allows users to simulate their movements in this environment with the help of wearable devices. Currently, VR technology is used primarily in the gaming industry. You could, however, integrate this technology into your marketing strategy in unique ways in order to attract customers.

In 2014, Coca-Cola brand used VR technology to increase brand awareness just before the start of the Football World Cup. They hosted an event at which they allowed guests to play for their favorite team in a virtual environment. The event was massively popular among football enthusiasts, and it enabled Coca-Cola to significantly increase their brand reach and sales.

As a car dealership, you can use VR technology to promote your brand, and while this sort of technology certainly isn't yet affordable for every dealership, I don't think it will be terribly long before it is. The VR technology I have seen used most provides a way to see the interiors of vehicles. Imagine the day when you can go for a test drive without going to the dealership! You could arrange a VR event and invite current or potential customers via social media. Provide virtual reality sets to your guests so they can enjoy driving the vehicles your dealership offers in different virtual settings. In all likelihood, your competitors haven't thought of this (yet).

## CHATBOTS

Many businesses have begun using chatbots to enhance their customer service. Chatbots are a digital tool built with Artificial Intelligence technology. These applications work without human intervention, pre-programmed to communicate with customers and make decisions on their own based on the direction in which a specific conversation goes. It's certainly possible to develop a strategy that includes chatbots for efficient communication, and you can take your dealership to new heights by incorporating chatbot technology into your social media strategy. Doing so will allow you to save resources while providing an excellent experience to your customers. You can integrate chatbots with different social media accounts to reply to messages and posts of customers.

One of the main benefits of incorporating chatbot technology is that a social media team typically works during standard business hours. Chatbots, however, operate seamlessly throughout the day (and night), allowing you to engage with customers who post content about your dealership or attempt to interact with your brand via messenger services after working hours or over the weekend. You cannot, however, leave everything to a chatbot. It's important to note that these automated systems *do not* reduce the need to have (human) social media managers on your team.

I once had a security system that used Chatbots as a way to replace the human connection between company and consumer, and I ran into an issue where they didn't send me the correct information. I was put on hold and prompted to press number one or five at least 10 different times and then repeat my entire issue once I was connected with a live agent. It was the worst experience because they never fixed the initial issue, and after months of calling (I called at least twice a month for five months, every time having to repeat myself even though they'd assured me that they "would make sure to update the notes on your account"), I finally canceled and went with a different provider and product altogether.

## FACEBOOK

Direct calling and Facebook ads are definitely my two favorite acquisition and retention approaches and the ones dealerships absolutely cannot be without (nor will they be able to be without them anytime soon).

Both Charles Maund and the other dealerships I now work with have so much success advertising on Facebook that I'll devote a large portion of this content to the strategies we've found most useful in that area as well as those I can advise you to save time and money by avoiding. Remember, when Charles Maund began working with an agency that specialized in Facebook advertising in 2013, I thought, "There's no way we're going to sell cars off of Facebook." I clearly remember how skeptical I was. This particular agency was running social media campaigns for 20 or so other companies at the time, but we were their first and only auto dealership. Because their founders had worked for Facebook before starting their own agency, they had unique insights into how best to successfully utilize the platform. However, since they'd never before partnered with a car dealership, mine and Dale's insights were necessary to most efficiently and effectively create successful campaigns. Interestingly, after working side-by-side with us for a few months and seeing the incredible potential Facebook ads had to bring in customers and sales to car dealerships, the agency switched their business model to one wherein they *only* work with auto dealerships. Andrew Street and partner Keith Turner of Dealer OMG have become both proven partners and great friends.

Throughout our initial meetings, I continued to ask, "Why can't we target customers based on their interest rate?" or "Why can't we target customers based on the model car they purchased?" It became clear that the approaches dealerships required to be able to be most effective on social media weren't being utilized, and by working together and combining the agency's knowledge of Facebook with my knowledge of vehicle sales and our dealership's customers, the ad campaigns began to take off.

One of the best suggestions I can make based on our experience is to get as much use as you can from each piece of content you create. As I mentioned previously, when you make a video that's more than a few minutes in length, you can break it up to create a series of videos.

STRATEGY WINS

**Get as much use as you can from each piece of content you create.**

THE UNFAIR ADVANTAGE

Facebook has several of benefits when it comes to dealership advertising.

## TARGETING

One of Facebook's greatest attributes as an advertising platform is that it allows businesses to specifically target who sees their ads. As an example, Charles Maund recently posted a live Facebook video because the Alexa app now pairs with the Toyota Avalon to allow customers to schedule service. The marketing manager and I wanted to show just how easy it is to schedule service at the dealership from an Avalon using Alexa. They then ran an ad with that video post and targeted Avalon customers, current dealership customers, friends of current dealership customers, and Toyota intenders (those shown via credit companies to have applied for a loan from a Toyota dealership in the previous six to twelve months). We got 9,000 views pretty quickly. You can't buy that sort of visibility for anywhere near that cost or speed anywhere else. To do a commercial like that on TV would require weeks of preparation and filming, not to mention thousands of dollars in cost and an inability to have any true control over or track who was seeing the ad content.

You can easily target customers who have bought a car from your dealership. Years ago, we had a salesperson who would, every time he sold someone a car, send a letter to that customers' neighbors that said, "Your neighbor just bought a Camry from us. Let me know if you are interested in a Toyota or have any friends who might be interested in one!" With Facebook, I don't have to go through the effort of crafting the letter, having it printed, having envelopes stuffed and addressed, paying for postage, and having no real idea if the recipient ever even opens the envelope. I can simply create an ad and target customers as well as friends of customers.

## RETARGETING

I'm a firm believer in retargeting anytime you can do it. It's incredibly inexpensive, and it's a targeted (pun intended), built-in follow-up. Almost everyone does it on any platform that has the necessary functionality in place. Facebook and YouTube are the platforms where we had the greatest success through retargeting. We put a Facebook pixel on every single page of our website and targeted anyone who visited the site as a whole with another ad. For next to nothing in the grand scheme of our budget, I could get in front of these same people again and again. We looked at users who visited specific pages as well. For example, if someone spent a good bit of time on the RAV4 page, we'd serve them up an ad featuring a RAV4 or similar vehicle.

With YouTube, if a visitor has been to our site, we can retarget them so that they'll always see our video or pre-roll. When a YouTube user is attempting to watch specific content, they are often forced to watch an entire commercial before accessing their desired content. Even I don't love that as a consumer, but but as a result I have found that I end up looking more into many of the brands that sponsor the ads as a result of viewing them.

The overall strategy is based on the frequency with which a user sees our brand. We were creating top-of-mind awareness so that anytime they're thinking, "I need a new car," subliminally, Charles Maund is the first dealership to pop into their head.

Facebook is a prime example of what we call "underpriced attention." Eight or nine years ago when we ran TV commercials with our phone number, the minute a commercial aired, my phone would ring. That doesn't happen anymore. The reach of TV has been heavily watered down because people simply aren't paying attention to the commercials (unless they're watching the Super Bowl). People are DVRing their favorite shows and fast-forwarding through commercials. We shifted into Facebook ads about five years ago, and over my last two years at the dealership, we slowly tripled our Facebook ads budget given our high level of success using the platform to reach customers. GoogleAdWords can also be an underpriced attention platform when you use specific, relevant, and underused keywords. The key words there are *specific, relevant,* and *underused.* When you're using relevant, popular keywords, the CPC can be as high as $15, which is completely opposite the $.01 video views we can generate through Facebook. Facebook reach combined with its high frequency allows you to reach a ton of people who are on their phone all the time. I mean, the average person spends four hours per day on Facebook!

When I left Charles Maund, we were at a point where we spent $30,000 per month on Facebook ads. For point of comparison, just one quality commercial will cost $20,000-$30,000. One strategy we've used when we do invest in a TV commercial is to cut it up into eight or nine videos and release them through Facebook, targeting different segments. That approach with a TV ad would cost an inordinate amount of money, and through Facebook, we can see what percentage of each video is being watched and retarget people who watch more than a certain percentage of a particular video.

For $1,000 I can generate 8,200 leads. When someone clicks on the link in the Facebook ad, we collect their information if they're interested in learning more about a particular vehicle. That's the CTA: if you'd like more info, give us your name and email address and/or phone number. Sometimes they'll be looking at a pre-owned vehicle and we'll re-target them with a similar vehicle. Most dealers are spending $20-$30 per lead, and worse, they're spending $500-$600 per customer acquisition. At Charles Maund, it costs—on average—$258 to sell a car. The margins speak for themselves.

When I leave a voicemail as myself, people call in and understandably ask to be connected to me. I learned I needed to train my phone staff to say, "Chris told me you'd be calling. Let me look up your information. It looks like he called you about your interest rate, and it looks like we have an opportunity to reduce that payment significantly. When can we get together to chat about it further?" The AutoMiner software makes it completely clear to my entire sales team who we called, when, and why so they are equipped to seamlessly handle the calls as they come in.

The AutoMiner also works brilliantly as a referral engine. Within the email marketing component, there's always an after-the-sale contact. There's a referral request wherein you say, "If I treated you right, please send your friends and family to me!" By the same token, I can create a Facebook ad and target everyone a salesperson has sold to with a video message that says, "Hey there! It's [insert name], and I sold you a car recently." They can go on to ask, "Did you know that every Toyota vehicle comes with [insert features]?" or something to that effect. There can be a Call to Action at the end to share the video with their friends and family as a referral or comment about what they love most about their new vehicle. We took that approach with several salespeople from different dealerships early on, and those salespeople ended up getting an enormous number of friend requests as a result.

We used big data to target not only our owner base but also everyone else's owner base. People think it's the dealerships selling everyone's data, but it isn't. I employed the same approach with voicemail marketing and targeting them on Facebook. We bought the data and target these customers on Facebook. We don't put the data into The AutoMiner because The AutoMiner only manages the data of actual customers— anyone who has purchased a vehicle from us or had their vehicle serviced by us. But we still use big data in order to generate thousands of clicks to our website as a result.

When you're approaching a completely cold audience (people who have never before heard of you), it can be effective to send an informational voice mail message or target them with an informational Facebook post. I'd be fully transparent about the fact that I'm targeting them and why. I'd say, "The reason you're seeing this video or receiving this message is that you financed a vehicle at a higher interest rate than you needed to. I'd love to show you how you can save money by either trading in your car or refinancing." I then show them the entire refinancing process. These types of videos get a significant reach for $.01 or $.02 per click. You can, by the end, acquire the customer for between $1 and $4 (after they see the first video, you have to invest to retarget them).

If you aren't using the following retargeting strategies on Facebook, you're missing out:

## TARGET A CUSTOMER'S FACEBOOK FRIENDS

I remember being told (by a top salesperson in his field) that, if you want to get sales using snail mail, you should send a letter to the neighbor of every customer you sell to, letting them know that someone in their neighborhood just bought a car from you and that you'd be happy to have them come chat with you about their car-buying needs. His thought process was in line with "keeping up with the Joneses." Once we fast-forwarded to the age of Facebook, I realized that you can now 10x that approach by uploading all the customers to whom you've sold or serviced a car in order to market to their friends and friends of friends. I was blown away by the results.

## USE FACEBOOK AS A FOLLOW-UP TOOL

I've always been a fan of follow-up, primarily because I know most people don't do it. Because of that, I've always believed that it was to my competitive advantage to be doing it. Now, the 6,000 to 10,000 clients the average dealer sees going to their website through their Facebook Pixel can be re-marketed to in order to offer them a special offer or more information about a vehicle they were already looking at.

## RE-TARGET CUSTOMERS WHO HAVE ALREADY ENGAGED

If you're already creating ads on Facebook, you need to re-target the customers who have engaged with your other ads. Those individuals are more likely in-market buyers today, and you should stay in front of them.

## RE-TARGET INTENDERS

People who are car-buying intenders or previous customers who may be in the ideal part of the car ownership cycle to begin generating interest in a new vehicle are audiences you must stay in front of.

## LINKED IN

Since the launch of The AutoMiner, I've spent lots of time doing B2B marketing. My goal is to connect with as many dealership GM's, owners, dealers, principals, and managing partners as I can so that when I post videos, the reach I get is targeted. As of this writing, I have 4,000 or so LinkedIn connections, and they're almost all members of the automotive industry. When I post videos, I can see how many people see that content. I'm trying to get their attention with that first video, and then I'll upload a new video, intended to grab their attention even further. Many people don't realize that you can boost targeted posts on LinkedIn just like you can on Facebook. For the Charles Maund Toyota professional LinkedIn page, we can choose to target business professionals aged 35 to 45 with content intended to engage them in a specific way.

LinkedIn is also a great way to promote job opportunities at your dealership. It's a cost-effective way of getting both customers *and* employees. It can be quite expensive to recruit new employees, and both Facebook and LinkedIn are great platforms to cost-effectively find great new talent.

Jamie Shanks wrote a book on social selling called *Social Selling Mastery: Scaling Up Your Sales and Marketing Machine for the Digital Buyer*. In the book, he details how to convert people into sales using LinkedIn specifically. When a lead comes in, it's often more effective to connect via LinkedIn in order to communicate with them. If they don't respond via email, you can connect with them more formally in order to get to know more about them and their needs. It's a good approach in terms of keeping things professional. LinkedIn tends to have a more professional "vibe" to it than the more casual, social one Facebook has. You don't necessarily want to be quite as goofy as you might be on Facebook.

I honestly don't use LinkedIn nearly as much as I should, but with The AutoMiner launching, it now has its own page and we're working on a content promotion strategy. For now, I post videos on my personal page first. When I did this most recently, the video quickly got 2,000 or so views. I've actually had more engagement on that video on LinkedIn than I did when I first pushed it out on my Facebook page. Facebook wants pages to pay to boost posts now, so the organic reach from them isn't nearly as high as it once was.

It's become harder to know who's genuine anymore on any social media platform because there's so much saturation, and everybody has an attitude of "I'm famous; I'm a celebrity; I'm an expert; I make millions of dollars." You don't really 100% know, but if you trust your gut, you'll find those who are genuinely doing really good, ethical things.

From a B2B perspective for fleet customers, you must be on LinkedIn, plain and simple. Never before in history has it been possible to identify and get into direct contact with the decision makers of a business you're interested in targeting. LinkedIn gives you the ability to message them *today*. You literally can simply look up the decision maker and then send them a message. Of course, sending the right message is important, but a simple, "Hi there, I sell fleet vehicles for your type of business at a reduced cost" is an easy way to open up the lines of communication. I've been able to put together multiple deals through LinkedIn simply by getting in contact with the decision maker directly.

## TIPS & TRICKS

Over the years, I've gleaned a few simple tricks to maximizing your dealership's ad budget and effectiveness. The truth is, it's not the extremely complicated strategies that end up making the biggest difference. It's the little tweaks that dealerships often overlook, thinking they're too small to have a big impact.

Some of my most effective tweaks:

- Seek out billboards that are unused to get the best deals.
- Give people a reason to be excited about receiving direct mail, voice mail, etc. because they know they are getting something of value from you.
- Don't use hashtags on all platforms.
- Be careful about your hashtags. The #WhyIStayed hashtag is used by women to share their experiences of domestic abuse. DiGiorno Pizza, not knowing about its actual context, used it to promote their pizza. It attracted a lot of criticism and many Twitter users bashed the company for their irresponsible and insensitive approach.
- Look for the images of vehicles competitor car dealer posts. If their customers show interest in that vehicle, it's possible that you can attract them by offering the same vehicle at discounted rates.
- Ensure that your marketing strategy is comprised of free as well as paid advertising methods. You can opt for cost-effective platforms such as social media sites for brand promotion.
- Your marketing campaign won't prove to be fruitful if you fail to properly select your target audience. The key to making any online marketing campaign fruitful is to choose your target audience first and then plan your marketing strategy accordingly.
- Your customer base should be your top priority. Do not assume on your own that a specific product is the top choice of your customers. Conduct customer surveys in person or via social media to understand the desires and requirements of your customers.
- The same goes for content marketing strategy. When you post any content on digital platforms, make sure it is relevant to the needs of your target audience and can keep them engaged.

- Partner with companies that sell auto parts. Not only will this campaign target your own customer base, you may also be able to sell your vehicles to the customer base of your partner. This way, you and your partner can attract more customers at half the advertising costs.
- Partner with complementary businesses such as carwashes. Several are already doing this quite successfully. The carwash provides free washes for life at any of their locations for anyone who purchases a car from a particular dealership. This partnership is prominently advertised both in the dealership and at the carwash.
- Although you should create content on current events, your website also needs evergreen content. Evergreen content doesn't need to be updated regularly. No matter how many years later viewers access this content, they'll find it beneficial. As a dealership, you can share tips about buying vehicles and other consistent information with your customers.

# MEASURE THE DATA

I live by the trial and error method. However, if you don't try something for long enough and truly measure how well it's working, you can't properly scale it, and you risk losing a lot of money to an ineffective strategy.

Unfortunately, simply creating unique content and sharing it with your followers isn't enough. You must also measure the impact of your overall marketing strategy. Too often, dealerships invest time and money coming up with a strategy that, in the end, doesn't benefit them. But they don't figure that out until it's too late.

When you plan your marketing strategy, you must clearly specify measurement parameters. These parameters will help you identify and measure the effects of a marketing campaign. A marketing plan can have different purposes, including visibility, lead generation, and an increase in visitors and customer engagement. Some businesses develop a creative marketing plan, but they forget to decide on key metrics before enacting that plan. Without well-defined KPIs (Key Performance Indicators), you can't expect to measure the impacts and performance of your marketing strategy. Your KPIs should be specified according to your goals.

Before you finalize your marketing plan, it's essential to think of performance indicators that'll work for you. These KPIs depend on your marketing goals. For instance, if you want to increase your customer base, the KPIs can be the number of likes, whereas if you want to retain customers, you can choose the number of comments and positive reviews by customers as your main KPIs.

There is no hard and fast rule that defines what your KPIs *should* be. The performance indicators vary with every business. If you have a marketing plan in place and are clear about your goals and overall mission statement, it'll be easier for you to define appropriate KPIs and develop your strategy in an efficient manner.

I recommend that dealerships execute a particular strategy for at least 90 days before determining whether or not it's viable and scalable. Sometimes, you'll launch a campaign and learn very quickly that it's not working, but you certainly can't base a campaign's long-term potential over its initial two-day performance. We used to change a lot of our strategy more often in the early days, but once we started seeing what approaches were working, we just kept doing them and slowly scaled them up.

MEASURE THE DATA

Execute a particular strategy for at least 90 days before determining whether or not it's viable and scalable.

THE UNFAIR ADVANTAGE

Use analytics tools to determine the efficacy of your marketing campaigns. If any campaign proves to be successful in meeting your objectives, you should continue with it. Otherwise you ought to revise and tweak your strategy so it better aligns with your customers' needs.

Before carrying out a marketing campaign, you must decide on the metrics you'll use to measure its degree of success. Metrics give you insight into whether or not your marketing campaign is effectively meeting your pre-specified goals. You can further use this information to enhance your overall marketing strategy and to target audience more effectively.

Also, it's not a recommended practice to manually measure the impacts of a marketing campaign. Tools such as PostPlanner, Canva, Buffer, Sprout Social, and Cyfe can help you both improve your social media activity and keep tabs on the impacts of your marketing efforts. There are several analytics tools you can use to evaluate the performance of your social media campaigns. Services such as Followerwonk, ViralWoot, and Google AnalyticScan use social media analytics tools to evaluate the performance of social media campaigns. Followerwonk, ViralWoot, Google Analytics, Quintly, Tailwind, Keyhole, Klout, and Audiense are some useful analytics tools that help you evaluate the performance of your social profiles. You can create automated reports for further evaluation.

There are different parameters you can use to analyze the efficacy of a marketing campaign, specifically a social media marketing campaign. It's important to track the number of followers of your page, profile visits, total views of your posts, number of comments on your posts, and user-generated content about your business. Make sure to separately measure the performance of each of your social media profiles. By doing that, if you notice that your Instagram profile isn't performing as well as your LinkedIn page, you'll be able to take effective steps to promote your business more effectively via Instagram.

Today, advertisers can use cutting-edge technology to boost their sales and revenue. On-demand platforms work with content delivery networks. A CDN is a collection of various servers that deliver content to users on the basis of their geo-location. These CDN servers allow businesses to track down their viewership in an efficient manner. Furthermore, advertisers don't need to pay any additional charges to access these statistics. We capture all website traffic from a dealership's website and retarget them everywhere. In one instance, for $692 I was able to retarget everyone who visited the dealership's website, and from that spend I was able to generate 53 leads and sell 12 cars.

The AutoMiner's integration with Facebook (and soon YouTube and Google Ads) allows us to see reporting on all of our ads specifically. It's cleaner reporting than what Facebook provides, and it's customized to show only what a dealership needs to see.

When it comes to direct mail, you can place a special code or phone number on the mailing in order to track callers as responders to a particular piece of mail. If you send out a voicemail and the phones start ringing off the hook, that's a pretty good indicator that your tactic worked. With Facebook campaigns, you can use The AutoMiner to grab the appropriate data and net 1000 clicks, but you also need to know how many of those people come into or call the dealership. With voicemail, we know exactly who calls us back because we have the recording of the original voicemail that was sent. We can look into the system and see who actually ended up translating into a sale. For Facebook tracking, I put a dealership's Facebook pixel onto their website, and anyone who visits the website is retargeted. They're generated as a lead into The AutoMiner, and then we can track those leads and see how many cars are sold off of it.

I can generate an actual ad campaign through The AutoMiner and send it through to Facebook. I only track click-throughs to our website, so I can see that a specific ad generated a certain number of clicks. While you may be thinking that The AutoMiner could end up replacing the need to have a human being managing Facebook, SMS, or GoogleAds campaigns, this really isn't true. As I've said, no effective marketing plan can be on full-on autopilot. The AutoMiner doesn't replace agency involvement; it simply makes it more effective and efficient. The more you can automate different aspects of your marketing efforts, the better it is for everyone involved. At the end of the day, somebody (or some tool) has to mine your data properly before getting it over to the agency or whomever else is creating your ad campaigns.

# THE AUTOMINER ADVANTAGE

Normally, a dealership has to ask the DMS to break down information in order to contact customers. It's incredibly time-consuming. Data-mining solutions fail for one or more reasons, including:

- Your sales team is too busy
- You don't have a process for your sales team to follow
- Your sales team hasn't bought in
- Your sales team is tired of rejection
- Your sales team isn't prepared
- Your sales team thinks it's too much work
- Your sales team members create notes but don't make the calls

I helped run one of the largest single point franchises in Texas, and I still ran into these issues, so thinking that any (or all) of them aren't present is simply putting your head in the sand.

We were not the only dealership struggling with this issue. When working with another dealership on their marketing recently, I asked them to send me a list of customers who had equity in their vehicle. The dealership manager sent a list three separate times, and each time I was able to poke holes in it based on the information in their actual database. It took two full days for them to send me a correct list. Dealerships do not have that kind of time to waste!

When I noticed that we had this issue several years ago, I had a conversation with my partner, James. I said, "Man, wouldn't it be great if we could just kind of create lists and sort customers' information really easy? I don't know why nobody's thought of this; why don't any of these CRM programs make it easier for dealerships?" That's where the conversation ended at that time. James left the dealership in 2015, but one day, I thought, "I'm gonna reach out to some tech groups just for the heck of it and see what can be done." I called around and found a company that could build the platform I'd envisioned. They said, "It'll take probably a month or two to build it."

Three years and a ton of money later, we had a prototype. And that prototype kept evolving. We kept tweaking it while using it in the dealership. We were basically building and molding it as necessary to serve our unique needs as a dealership.

A couple of months later I called James and said, "I have an idea. This is what I've created so far." I showed him the program, and he agreed it was a great idea. We got his dad (and my mentor), Jim, involved to take it to the next level. The three of us became partners. We wrote up an agreement, signed it, formed a company, and went from there. It slowly began growing, and as we've refined it to be better and better, we've been able to service more customers as a result. As we incorporated newer technologies such as SMS, voicemail, and email, our capabilities in terms of targeting people on Facebook evolve every single day.

Three years ago, we were just trying to create an effective sales assistant, and as of 2018 we've begun licensing The

AutoMiner for use by other dealerships. It's actually hard to find great marketing people. Charles Maund Toyota has three BDCs (Business Development Centers), which most dealers don't even have in-house. They work hand-in-hand with the marketing department. Once the marketing team determines what kind of lists they want to target and what campaigns they want to run, they deploy the process to a BDC. There is a new car, used car, and service-focused BDC, and they're each constantly trying to develop more business or generate new business from current customers.

Before creating The AutoMiner, we had to manually pull the data out of our DMS and upload it to Facebook. I wanted a process where we could simply press a button and the correct data would be sent to Facebook. So that's what we created. We can now segment customer history by the type of loan they have, the model they purchased, or whatever other criteria we'd like. We can send the data directly to Facebook via an API, and we can now do that for our SMS messages as well.

In mid-2018, I transitioned from being the general sales manager at a mega dealership to running The AutoMiner full-time. Over the previous three years, we'd constantly honed the tool as we used it, and it was time to let it be all that it's capable of being for other dealerships as well. My biggest focus has always been retention—both sales and service. We had over 100 bays in our service environment at Charles Maund. I wanted them to be full from the time we opened until the time we closed, and I firmly believed that The AutoMiner was a key player in making that happen as efficiently as possible. We spent those first three years watching the software break, tweaking it, and finding different ways to use it effectively. I've always thought, "Wouldn't it be easier if I knew I could bring these customers back two or three years from now and sell them a new vehicle?" This is where the "lazy" aspect of my personality comes into play. How can we do something as efficiently and effectively as possible? Much to my delight, we ended up with a product even greater than I'd initially anticipated.

Many dealerships sell a lot of cars but don't have anyone following up with customers they can sell more cars or service to. "Where's my sales assistant?" was the question I found myself continuing to ask myself. We didn't have service assistants or sales assistants. Sometimes, dealerships do have sales or service assistants, but they're afraid to make phone calls to begin with or just don't have time. That's a problem that The AutoMiner solved.

Whether they're doing their proactive marketing themselves or not, dealerships constantly get calls from sales and marketing agencies that want to help with advertising efforts. The biggest challenge we faced when it came to partnering with these agencies (including the ones we were already partnered with) was that, in order for any agency to take effective action, we had to be able to provide them with properly segmented data. Without that data, neither the agency nor we could could effectively target ad campaigns, make phone calls, leave voice mails, send out SMS messages, emails, or direct mail.

THE AUTOMINER ADVANTAGE

**It's critical that dealerships be able to segment their database properly.**

THE UNFAIR ADVANTAGE

It's critical that dealerships be able to segment their database properly. After all, if you create a list of people to target, that list is no good if it has customers on it who should not be on it, and is missing customers it should have. For years, the only way to make sure we had a correct list (and the only way many dealers still have to ensure that they create a correct list) was to manually create it. That took an enormous amount of time.

Charles Maund's main customer database has 120,000 people in it, but The AutoMiner only manages the data of actual customers—individuals who have either purchased a car from the dealership or had service with them because we know we can legally target them through advertising.

I can quickly and efficiently send a pre-recorded voicemail to everyone who has financed a vehicle within the last 12 to 36 months *and* made at least twelve payments on time. I can actually help improve their financial situation by helping them trade in their vehicle and lowering the payment on a new vehicle. I once sent that kind of message, and within 30 minutes had someone drive in to the dealership, and we sold them a car. There's not a single company through which you can put a TV or radio ad up that quickly and get that kind of response. I literally can deploy a message, and within a couple of minutes of sending it out our phones are ringing. I'll have 150 people call me back within minutes.

I typically sent these sorts of messages via voicemail, not text, because I don't want to overuse SMS. SMS messaging is primarily used for service-related communication. You can easily text someone too often, causing them to unsubscribe, and I'd rather use SMS to communicate with our customers on servicing their current vehicle than selling them a new one.

One feature I'm building into the application came from an experience my daughter had. She and my wife area always selling things on Facebook Marketplace, and recently she listed something, someone said they were on their way to purchase it, and then an hour later they messaged to say they were no longer interested. My daughter was then able to send a message to everyone who had said they were interested, letting them know the item was again available. Within a minute, she had five people ready to come pick up the item.

One thing I saw all the time was, we'd meet with a customer and not be able to make a deal for one reason or another. Or, I could see that a specific car had been on five or six different test drives, but I wasn't sure why it didn't sell. It would have been great if we could have filtered for customers who had test-driven a car and not been able to purchase it because we couldn't come to an agreement on price, but then there was a price drop or rebate available. There's no application out there that segments data like this, and it creates so much opportunity! Today, dealerships can use the application to target a Facebook ad to all customers who have purchased, say, an Avalon letting them know that a new model has come out and describing all of its newest features.

Charles Maund is underneath a freeway overpass. If you're driving by, you're likely going to miss it. There's no exit ramp. You truly have to know where we are. So when I had downtime, I was always calling people. I say, "Just pick up the phone and start dialing." However, before The AutoMiner, it would take me a couple of hours just to create the list of people to call! I had salespeople who wanted to call all the people with Spanish last names, and when a need like that arose, we called our developers and had that filter added.

Another benefit of The AutoMiner is that car brands co-op use of it. They'll pay individual dealerships to advertise so it's basically free money for the dealership. At the end of the day, Toyota doesn't care from which dealerships they sell cars; they care about selling more cars overall than they did the previous year. So, if a dealership has access to and is successfully using The AutoMiner, the overarching brand may be willing to pay for much of the advertising that is done, knowing that it's specific, targeted, and profitable.

One dealership I work with is using The AutoMiner only for service right now. If a dealership doesn't have a BDC or service retention center where they're actively trying to set up appointments in order to fill up their service drive, The AutoMiner helps with that. Our BDC actually reaches out via SMS, letting customers know that it's time for them to come in for service, and they know who to reach out to because of the dealership data in The AutoMiner. Soon, we'll have a new layer of functionality in play whereby, when a customer calls in for service, The AutoMiner will recognize who the customer is and say, "Hi Jen! Are you calling about your Corolla?" The customer says Yes and the system then asks, "When would you like to schedule service?" Artificial Intelligence takes over and gets the service appointment scheduled. It frees up a human being to be doing tasks that are more important to be done with human interaction such as sales and follow-up.

With The AutoMiner, a dealership can segment customers by income as well as all other kinds of parameters. You can target customers who bought a car from you with a high interest rate (between 10% and 26%) more than 12 months ago. The first time I did that, one of our salespeople came up to me and said, "Man, I'm so happy that you you did. I sold four cars, and that got me to my bonus."

Your salespeople should be making these calls already, but the voicemail marketing takes time out of the equation. The AutoMiner generates it instantaneously. I spoke to a dealership general manager recently who has a generic data mining solution. I asked him to see the engagement rate. It looked as though his salespeople had generated about 400 phone calls for the whole month and made two appointments as a result. I said, "That took an entire month. The AutoMiner will take care of that whole task in an hour."

Instead of generating two appointments, The AutoMiner made twice as many calls, resulting in 40 appointments. The GM had his "aha moment" right then and there. Why keep your salespeople busy doing busywork when you can help them generate real customer engagement, sell some vehicles, and then give them other opportunities to take additional action throughout the month. Just as it is with any other business, if you spend all day pushing content to the wrong demographic, you're working your butt off but will have nothing to show for it. I use the same approach with voicemail. When someone's lease is about to expire, I'll leave a message for them to call me. If I sent this same message via email, I might get a 2-4% open rate. It's really hard to get engagement there. Using The AutoMiner, I'll send out 3,000 voicemail messages and perhaps 10% of those people will call me back.

It's certainly not imperative that dealers use The AutoMiner, but when it comes to social media, the tool takes a *lot* of human time as well as mistakes out of the equation. It also hooks into Facebook to prove a dealership's ad spend. There is no DMS in existence right now that can segment customer data as easily as The AutoMiner can. And because it connects directly to Facebook via an API, dealerships are able to be crystal clear on their ad spend.

For dealerships that license The AutoMiner, we can create a 12-month strategy whereby they'll be able to have a small ads budget and even focus only on retention to start if that's their preferred approach. If you've never done any Facebook ads before and/or don't have an agency you're working with, The AutoMiner acts as a solid, basic starter kit for those campaigns. From there, if dealerships want The AutoMiner's media agency to do some more creative for them such as direct mail, we can handle that. An in-house graphic designer will still be incredibly beneficial, but for Facebook, YouTube, and GoogleAds, The AutoMiner will have pre-created, proven design templates that dealerships can simply customize with pertinent information. The person in charge of marketing at a dealership can decide which graphics they want to use for a particular campaign, customize them, and roll them out to a specific segment of their database.

If The AutoMiner is handling SMS messaging combined

with voicemail, it will send an SMS to a customer and then do the follow-up with a voicemail saying something to the effect of, "Hey there! I sent you a text message the other day about a new offer we have. Call me if you'd like to discuss your options further." Once that customer calls back, the virtual answering service takes over. What this is allowing is for dealerships to truly filter out leads that aren't solid while allowing their salespeople to focus all of their time and attention on the leads that *are* solid.

To demonstrate how effective The AutoMiner is proving to be, for approximately $5,000 I know I can get a couple hundred customers into a dealership's service department. If those appointments are generating between $100 and $200 per ticket on the low-end, $100 times 200 generates $20,000 from that $5000 investment. If The AutoMiner can help a dealership sell 10 or 20 cars with an average margin of $700 on a new car and $1500 on a pre-owned car, that's a fantastic return. If the customer then purchases an extended warranty on top of that, the profit margin only continues to go up. It's almost a no-brainer to start there because, when dealerships are investing their full budget into TV commercials, spending $10,000 to $25,000 per commercial, they're investing upwards of $100,000 per year to sell perhaps 20 or 30 cars.

When I initially developed the application, it was to drive more business to Charles Maund Toyota. At the time, Toyota was making a big push in the area of service retention, and I thought, "Wait a minute. What about our sales retention? What do those numbers look like?" I recognized that we had to get that number up as well. I knew that, three years in the future, there would be another Toyota dealership within a few miles of us, so we needed to do a better job at retaining our customers so we'd be ahead of the curve. Sure enough, we were able to do that. It's the little tweaks that make a big difference.

The AutoMiner would work brilliantly for RV, boat, and motorcycle sales and service as well. There's simply no other tool out there that markets to customers this efficiently, and the way The AutoMiner methodology is applied is the same, whether a dealership is selling cars, boats, or motorcycles. A dealership is mining its own customer base and positioning themselves to be able to send those customers text messages, voicemails, or targeted ads on Facebook.

It removes time from the equation. A dealership can now do in five minutes what used to take days. Through prescribed messages and re-targeting, a dealership can go from marketing idea to inception to execution in just a few minutes and know that the message will hit their customer between seven and ten times within that month. That's never before been possible—the ability to so efficiently target customers at a fraction of the cost of doing it via TV and radio.

I began working with a dealership to incorporate The AutoMiner into their business plan a few months ago. They were netting approximately $800,000 per month, and we've already gotten them to $1.1 million per month. I truly believe that, if they continue to apply the strategies I've shown them, they'll get to 1.5 million dollars a month before long.

A dealership I recently visited had a pretty low engagement rate for the DMS they were using. They were generating approximately 150 phone calls in an entire month, resulting in only two appointments. That didn't seem like good engagement to them or to me! I applied The AutoMiner and personally trained their sales people how to effectively handle sales calls. Within the hour, we had generated 100 callbacks, 20 appts, and sold a car.

# AFTERWORD

**M**arketing platforms and approaches continue to evolve across all industries, however basic sales principles haven't changed in hundreds of years. Make sure people know who you are, what you do, and why they should buy from you. Stay in front of your customers after they drive off the lot with their new car (and even if they don't). Be involved in your community and genuinely assist those in it. Get extremely honest about what your marketing strategy is, how well it's working, and how you can improve it. Know your goals. Be able to measure your performance against them. And then be prepared to do what's necessary to exceed them going forward.

After countless years working to hone the marketing efforts at Charles Maund as well as partnering with other dealerships to help take their marketing strategies to the next level, I've been able to draw one undeniable conclusion: if you stick to the basics and do them well, you'll be properly setup to have the unfair advantage.

# ABOUT THE AUTHOR

When Chris Martinez entered the car sales industry in 2003, he had no definitive sense of direction. Even with successful mentors, his growth was organic and he had to make his own way in an increasingly competitive and difficult environment. He had to fall, get up and fall again. He had to make mistakes, learn from them and make new ones.

Chris set out to be the number one salesperson and receive a respectable paycheck in order to feed his family, never realizing that he could earn $20,000-$25,000 a month selling cars. He's proof that you don't have to be the greatest salesperson in the world, you only have to be willing to learn and apply yourself.

Now a co-partner of The AutoMiner software platform and a member of the board of The Automotive Partners (www.TheAutomotivePartners.com), he intends to globally disrupt the automotive space. Chris is passionate about teaching eager-to-learn salespeople as well as dealership managers how to think about and approach both current and prospective customers differently in order to consistently reach (and crush) their marketing and sales goals.

facebook.com/ChrisJMartinezatx

twitter.com/chrisjmartinez4

instagram.com/chrisjmartinezatx

## ALSO BY CHRIS J. MARTINEZ

Driving Sales: What It Takes to Sell 1000+ Cars Per Month

The Drive to 30: Your Ultimate Guide to Selling More Cars than Ever

# BREAKING NEWS...

Chris has joined the board of The Automotive Partners (www.TheAutomotivePartners.com) with the intent of globally disrupting the automotive space. For more information on his products and consulting opportunities, please visit either of his websites:      www.chrisjosephmartinez.com      or www.TheAutoMiner.com

Made in the USA
San Bernardino, CA
31 December 2018